THE PUBERTY TREE

Books by D.M. Thomas

POETRY

Personal and Possessive (1964)
Penguin Modern Poets 11
    with D.M Black & Peter Redgrove (1968)
Two Voices (1968)
Logan Stone (1971)
The Shaft (1973)
Love and Other Deaths (1975)
The Honeymoon Voyage (1978)
Dreaming in Bronze (1981)
New from the Front
    with Sylvia Kantaris (1983)
Selected Poems (1983)
The Puberty Tree: New & Selected Poems (1992)

TRANSLATIONS

Akhmatova: *Selected Poems* (1979, 1985)
Yevtushenko: *A Dove in Santiago* (1982)
Pushkin: *The Bronze Horseman and Other Poems* (1982)
Pushkin: *Boris Godunov* (1985)

NOVELS

The Flute-Player (1979)
Birthstone (1980)
The White Hotel (1981)
Russian Nights:
    Ararat (1983)
    Swallow (1984)
    Sphinx (1986)
    Summit (1987)
    Lying Together (1990)
Flying in to Love (1992)

MEMOIR

Memories & Hallucinations (1988)

D.M. THOMAS

The Puberty Tree

NEW & SELECTED POEMS

BLOODAXE BOOKS

ISBN: 1 85224 200 0

First published 1992 by
Bloodaxe Books Ltd,
P.O. Box 1SN,
Newcastle upon Tyne NE99 1SN.

PR6070
.H58
P8
1992

Bloodaxe Books Ltd acknowledges
the financial assistance of Northern Arts.

Cover printing by J. Thomson Colour Printers Ltd, Glasgow.

Printed in Great Britain by
Cromwell Press Ltd, Broughton Gifford, Melksham, Wiltshire.

*To the memory of
Harold and Amy Thomas,
my parents, and for
Lois Embleton, my sister.*

Acknowledgements

This book includes poems from the following collections by D.M. Thomas: *Penguin Modern Poets 11* (Penguin, 1968), *Two Voices* (Cape Goliard, 1968), *Logan Stone* (Cape Goliard, 1971), *The Shaft* (Arc, 1973), *Love and Other Deaths* (Paul Elek, 1975), *The Honeymoon Voyage* (Secker & Warburg, 1978), *Dreaming in Bronze* (Secker & Warburg, 1981) and *News from the Front*, a collaboration with Sylvia Kantaris (Arc, 1983); the poems by Sylvia Kantaris from *News from the Front* are available in her *Dirty Washing: New & Selected Poems* (Bloodaxe Books, 1989).

For the new and uncollected poems in the last section, acknowledgements are due to the editors of *Encounter* and *Transatlantic Review* who first published some of these poems, and to Five Seasons Press for *In the Fair Field*.

Contents

TWO VOICES
(1968)

Unknown Shores
(after Théophile Gautier)

Okay, my starsick beauty! –
blue jeans and tilting breasts,
child of Canaverel –
where would you like to go?

Shall we set set course for Mars,
or Venus's green sea,
Aldebaran the golden,
or Tycho Brahe's Nova,
the moons of Sagitta,
or Vega's colonies?

School-minching, bronze Diane,
bane of the launching-pads –
I may not ask again:
wherever you would go

my rocket-head can turn
at will to your command –
to pluck the flowers of snow
that grow on Pluto, or
Capella-wards, to pluck
the roots of asphodel?

I may not ask again:
where would you like to go?

Have you a star, she says,
O any faithful sun
where love does not eclipse?
...(The countdown slurs and slips).
– Ah child, if that star shines,
it is in chartless skies,

I do not know of such!
But come, where will you go?

Private Detentions

Here, girls, you sat, all but the dry, the purl-and-plain,
Collars awry, crumpled, pens dribbling 'I must not'
(Do, commit something or other) again and again:

Long legs crossed out of the desk, disdaining
The childish task – nylon, elegant, nubile,
Cool laddered dignity. Or great and lusty, generous
Christmas-joint legs, enlapping the puritan desks in style.

Detained and detaining, dreamy in their jukebox bliss,
Married to Paul or Ringo, dead to me; but others, dear
Moon-nymphs, enrapt in sly ceremonies

Here, alone with their nicelooking, friendly master.
– My fans or my priestesses,
And I the Sacred King whose lopped limbs, and lonely,
Faceless head with clotted spread-out tresses

They will send bobbing down a careless stream
At the year's end.
                    In some eyes, apathy;
In some, a resentful and sadistic gleam –

Harridans muscled for battle and blowsy, full of
A contempt my indiscipline has earned,
Their weapons, dumb insolence, jeers, a sudden muttered
'*Piss off!*' (then gasps of mirth) while my back is turned.

And always a ghost of love in the crippled air.
Alone, 'Your lessons *bore* me!' one rasped,
                    riddling my guts with her hatred.
Then cried. And my hand *must* not, *must* not, touch her hair.

A Lesson in the Parts of Speech

Loraine (my Proper but improper darling),
with all these chalked and innocent-eyed Abstractions,
with fear, desire, with jealousy, with pain,
I love
the things about you (Common but uncommon),
eyes, lips, hair, fingers, breasts and smiles and bottom,
blouse, skirt, suspenders, sweater, stockings, shoes

– for they are You, my one and only pronoun,
my slyly Personal, my unpossessed Possessive!
How queerly You, Demonstrative last night,
can sit, now, lost among your friends, Indefinite,

silent, anonymous, maddening, discreet,
concentrated, withdrawn from me, allowing
just the subtlest smile to play as I write up 'red',
our private joke; your genial body purrs
as you stretch your heavy limbs, back in the desk,
tight as a nun, arms folding warm to chest,
reserved, self-owned, and taking notes though bored.

Deep in the past, last night, we clung, we kissed,
tangled, confused the first and second person,
petted, then did your homework, frenchkissed again,
though when it came to the final, explosive verb,
you shut your self, in passive mood, and tense;
and seeing you in the class,
inviolate in fresh school-blouse, so serenely
escaping always into the future, the finite
so impossible to make infinitive,
in impotent, baffled fury I would plunge

wantonly, completely, here, now,

in through up under unto and beyond
above relationship of place or time or...

      But
(and this our accepted, clean and cold conjunction,
the word that separates us and attracts us)

all is determined in our complex sentence.
The bars of our open prisons call us back
from our brief, touching forays to the woods,
where planned ejaculations missed their mark.
You look up, meet my eyes. Heart thumps like a gong.
Your gaze is tender, teasing, swift. Mine says:
and oh! and oh! and oh!
                    till that time come again...
and yours: *hey nonny nonny!*

The Eumenides

The thing that worries me about
   the kind of people to whom
   the really terrible, o-so-shuddering things happen,
like
getting electrocuted in the bath or
haplessly plummeting off an Atlantic cliff
   (reaching right over for
   the last
   blackberry)
four hundred feet falling falling onto spiny uprushing rocks –
or having one's child raped and murdered in a wood,

is

that in their firm-built houses they
spent similarly pleasant dullish evenings reading about
   the kind of people to whom
   the really terrible things happen,
like,
   cancer of the bowels,
   a sliced off face in a machine,
   finding one's child raped and slaughtered in a wood.

Missionary

A harsh entry I had of it, Grasud;
the tiny shuttle strained to its limits
by radiation-belts, dust-storms,
not to mention the pitiless heat which
hit it on plunging into the atmosphere
– its fire-shield clean vaporised; and then,
on landing, the utter cold and stillness
of a mountain-slope, cedar trees and
what they call
snow. As I went numbly through the
routine I could do in my sleep –
mentalising myself, smothering
my body and the shuttle in a
defensive neutrino-screen, hiding them
securely in the snow,
I looked up and, between the branches
of the cedars, could see
the mother-ship sliding away through
the dark, like an unfixed star, westwards
to its other destinations: that was
the worst moment of all, Grasud! I'd have
called it back! So lonely! such an alien
world they'd left me in. Goodbye, Lagash!
goodbye, Theremon! fare well! (But no
voice now even to make a gesture against
the silence.)
           Then the agonisingly slow
descent, towards the village,
my spirit dark, already missing
not only Theremon and Lagash, but
that other friend, my body's familiar
chemistry. By now I felt my
vaunted courage ebbing, Grasud; I think
those years of training
alone forced me to go on, into the village,
into the houses, inns, into
– after much vain searching – a ripened
womb; there superseding
(not without a pang) its foetus-spirit.

How black that airlock,
after the six suns of our own system,
I needn't tell you. Even space,
in recollection, seemed a blaze of
supernovas. But I settled to my task,
wrestling to get on terms with carbon
compounds fearsomely different from
the synthetic ones I'd practised in.
Of course, as I was born and the years
passed, it seemed as natural to go
on man's two legs as on our Vardian
limbs. But when these pains eased,
one far bitterer grew: my seeds were cast
on stony ground; the more
I exhorted,
– the more I spoke, obliquely, of
the many mansions of our Vardian
Commonwealth, and of the place
that could be theirs – the more it
seemed those simple, instinctive creatures
lied, stole, slandered, fornicated,
killed...Grasud, how often, sick with
failure, only the words of Vrak
sustained me – 'a world lies in your hands.'
That was the time he
sent for the three of us when
all ears were ringing with the news of
the three life-planets found in
NDT 1065. If we had hopes,
we masked them. His words to us, for
all that's happened, I'll hoard always.
'Thoorin, Lagash, Theremon,' I hear him
saying, 'I'm sending *you*...you're young,
but this is what you've trained for, bio-
enlightenment. You've done well.'
And then – 'a world lies in your hands.'
So, Grasud, I toiled. In the end
I tried too hard; the time of space-
rendezvous was almost come. Anyway,
they killed me. I loved them, and they
killed me.

Yes, it was hard,
as you can well imagine,
on the return-journey, to avoid feeling
the faintest warp of
jealousy, as Theremon and
Lagash talked with
the happy emissaries of their
planets. – What does Vrak say? He is
kind, promises – after this loathsome
rest – another
chance, though not of course on that
planet. My 'inability' (he avoids
the word failure) to raise them
ethically to the point where we could
safely announce ourselves, proves, he
says, there's no point trying again
for a few thousand years. Meanwhile,
he suggests, maybe some of my words
will start to bear fruit...He is kind!
His last words were 'Forget about it,
Thoorin; enjoy your stay on
Atar.' Forget!
with the relaxed faces of my friends a
perpetual thorn!

Tithonus

And finally, ladies and gentlemen, perhaps in his quiet way
As exciting as many of our other exhibits,
Just group around and let me introduce you to
Our very first immortal *homo sapiens*.
Yes, here we have – but a word of caution, sir,
These tubes are delicate – the first *immortal*.
Let that word chime. Forget Jesus, forget
– Well, all the other man-gods of pre-history,
And fix your eyes instead on Edgar L. Cummings
As he floats here, bottled greyly in solution.
Death, Thou art Dead!
And isn't that typical scientific hooh-hah for something
So unimpressive – a mere pulsing sponge!
I don't blame you – But believe me when I say
That all Man's dreams of immortality,
– Penny for old Charon, them pearly gates,
Or some lotus-isle where falls not rain or hail –
Are here made coldly but thrillingly *fact*.
He just can't die!...– oh, barring some cosmic disaster.
Our Institute, you've seen, 's impregnable –
Fire-proof, bomb-proof, radiation-proof,
Sterilised; and when in a few billion billion years
Our sun threatens to blow up, he'll be whipped off
Like all the rest, to some more genial star.

Professor Wiggins will perhaps fill you in on
His case-history later – you can see
She's rather busy fussing over his welfare as usual!
Miss Wiggins, my colleague in the Department of Tithonics,
Was actually present twenty years ago,
In student capacity, when Professor Joseph performed
The historic excision. Briefly though: Edgar L. Cummings,
Born 1961, transfigured, so to speak, 2025
While dying, in coma, of arterio-sclerosis;
No relative surviving to worry about names,
Re-christened Tithonus, after an old Greek story
Which you will find briefly summarised on this plaque.
Unfortunately we can't provide an Eos,
Unless indeed Miss Wiggins – good EVENING, professor! –

Could be said to fill that category...She certainly clucks
Tenderly over him all hours of the day and night,
Spends less and less time at her East Side apartment,
Burns midnight fluorescence rivalling the splendour
Of her own auburn – *Why Dawn, I believe you're BLUSHING!*
Well, well – ! many a true word in jest, folks!
You'll bear me out, we've *proved* a real Heart beats
Under that tall and intellectual white,
That those spiky heels take the strain of Feminine passions!...
What's that? you'll get me later?...I'll look forward...!
Seriously, ladies and gentlemen, I know the question
You all must be dying to pose: in what queer sense
Can this blob of matter be called a human being,
Whether Tithonus or Edgar L. Cummings.
I answer: in the *only* sense: he thinks,
He feels himself to be; a continent,
Lapped everywhere by our amniotic flood,
He contains the mystery of his mystery,
Is infinitely more important to himself
Than all the infinitely more important cosmos
He only senses over a few square inches.
All that he's lost was excrescence – desirable,
To see, hear, move, speak – but not essential;
You lose a nail – not YOU; your legs – a pity;
But YOU remain, clenched in the brittle skull.
Here fed with tubers, that's the only difference.

Take a crane-fly wandering in from the river,
Settling on a door you've sprayed with paint.
One leg goes, in the frenzy to escape
– Two more – a wing – thick pencil scrawls
Grotesque millimetres away; now it knows
Not even God could separate paint from crane-fly
And leave enough of the latter. So it subsides,
Despairing. When you come along – my God, the paint! –
You expect it to welcome the tenderly offered rag,
The quick-crunch-and-it's-over. But no, it fights!
It tries to cringe. Not that it has any illusions
About ever getting away from this obscenity, it knows
The kindness of your gesture, but it just CAN'T
But try to protect its tiny brain from your pity.
Its little ego shrieks silently, LEAVE ME INTACT!

20

YOU DON'T KNOW HOW VITAL I AM.
Here, in this case, we've kept that ego intact.
I think I used the word excision,
As though what we cut *out* was expendable;
Call it rather a vast *amputation*
Of the body hacked clear away from the brain.
The *man* remains: meditates, desires, remembers.

Just to prove our point, watch now while Miss Wiggins
Stimulates a memory-cell. (Don't worry, he likes it;
Even when we happen to hit on a *bad* memory
He still enjoys the emotive exercise.)
Now...Watch...Keep one eye on the electro-
Encephalograph – WOOSH! See how the pencil goes
– Boy! – shooting up and up in fantastic hieroglyphics;
We've obviously hit on something pretty big.
That cell-twitch we gave him means he's now re-living
– Down to the very colours, textures of garments –
A moment in his past: living it more *intensely*
Almost, in that memory-cell, than he did at the time.
A green coat *feels* itself slipping to the floor!
Maybe he's walking down the lane with his first girl,
Stepping carefully over a puddle, the scent of rain
Mixing with hers, while a blackberry branch whips
Across his leg, or maybe bending over a cot,
Yellow, with elephants pasted on it,
Where his son's fighting for breath against pneumonia.
Here's where the absence of speech, etcetera,
Proves a barrier. We never get through to him, or vice versa.
This memory is obviously emotional, but whether
Lust, anger, fear – your guess is as good as ours.
Our stubborn de-cipherers will wrestle with it
Seeking as always some clue to find the verbal
Equivalent, break the code. It's a helluva problem, *but* –
Sooner or later they'll do it.
The last twenty years, of course, haven't been exactly rich
In memories, except of his own thought-processes
(These violent scribbles certainly relate back to
An earlier period.)
                      How far, you ask, is he
Aware of his situation? Well, obviously
He *can't* be aware of it at all, lacking

The normal apparati of discovery.
He only knows the contiguous bloodwarm
Solution, and our various probes – but this
Again is relative; aren't we, too, blissfully
Ignorant of our environment, outside
The (compared with infinity) contiguous
Galaxies a billion light-years away?
I admit the idea seems rather gruesome at first,
But he's happy because he *himself* exists.
'*Ay, but to die, and go we know not where!*'
– That's something he'll NEVER have to experience.
I hope and believe he'd thank us – no, that's an under-
Statement – if he could,
And say moreover how proud he is being
Our proto-immortal, paving the way for ALL
To escape even three days' extinction. What a niche
In history! Why, may I end by making the outrageous
Suggestion that already our grateful Tithonus
Is gropingly beginning to sense
The presence somewhere '*out there*' of a Miss Wiggins,
As she bends over: *senses* the auburn angel
Who watched Prof. Joseph roll back the stone
Before the stone was needed? That may sound a crazy
Hypothesis; Dr Reiner, our E.S.P. expert,
Reckons ten thousand years at least before
Our guest starts to develop his 'sixth sense',
But I've an idea this may be under-estimating
The powers of human adaptability.

Hera's Spring

*Missing his noisy play around the
house, and remembering the time was no
doubt near, she hurried out, unkempt as
she was, and found him at last, pale-faced
and tearstained, hunched on the weir bank — no
fishing-rod in sight — plunged in himself,
his pain. With a motherly tenderness
she wiped his eyes with her skirt-hem; she
knew; she gently questioned him; and said:*

Believe me, dear, though it will seem strange
to you, I have wept too for all these
things you mention — and others that may-
be have not yet started to haunt you
again. Do you recall, for instance,
the dark coppery flowers on the low
trees? the waterfalls, or methane-falls
— call them what you like — leaping off cliffs?
the strong, live winds, and violet sky
flashing with great clouds? And I expect
you have walked many a time with your
husband on those mountain-slopes as bright
as metal, with thunder laughing in
the ground, and clear red flame exploding
above you? I know *I* have — though with,
as it happens, a wife beside me
— a dear woman...I too have been there,
Jeserac; a terribly long time
ago, but it's still precious to me.

Today isn't the time to convince
you that these eroded hills, blue sky,
green woods, not to mention the speckled
fish you like catching, are themselves not
unbeautiful...this first day, you've a
right to feel desperate. I recall
myself (though how many others in
between!) writhing in the ammonia-
snow I'd always thought of as home, and
was to again – tormented by the
globe your mind is filled with, shrieking at
my sisters to leave me in peace! Poor
mites, they ran off and told everyone
that a yanu was inside me! – This,
darling, was near Procyon, the light
your father taught you to find last night.

– Oh, don't think I don't understand; it's
the *beings* you gave yourself in love
to – not moons or cliffs! And the dull ache
of this you must expect never to
wholly leave you. How often one finds
oneself wondering – and the worst of it's
being completely unable to
share your dark thoughts with anyone else –
where is, say, Kersti? – a granddaughter
I once had somewhere in Boötes;
in which of the far-flung micro-files
of our cosmic city Diaspar
is that beloved pattern crystallised;
and where will she – or he– emerge again?
Yet one knows there can be no answer.
Only the dumb Selector knows that.

Still, it's the way of Hera's Spring; we
have to count our blessings. – I see *that*
too hasn't come back yet, dear! It would
soon, so I may as well remind you.
Ages and ages ago, on this
very planet (in re-emerging
here, we've come home, in the deepest sense),
men, who had previously 'died', as

24

though they were cattle or sheep, found out
the secret of immortality.
...Still doesn't bring it back? – Just vaguely!
Well, anyway, after they'd finished
rejoicing, they found that, after all,
the threatening shears were things they couldn't
do without. It's said the daffodils
withered in the poets' verses; nothing
seemed beautiful when nothing would pass
away! – in fact, they found the prospects
so deadly they clamoured for death to
be restored. Instead, their scientists
thought up a middle way, called *Hera's
Spring,* (I don't know who gave it that name).
But it came from the way Hera, 'queen
of the heavens' (you've heard of her in
this world) renewed her virginity,
that is her purity, each year, by
bathing in the spring of Canathos.
It fits. The spring we step into is
the frozen heart of a crystal, from
which we emerge, having just held our
breaths, maybe a million years later.

This first time is the worst, Jeserac
dear – your homesickness, if you like, is
focused, not radiated. When you
have had, like me, almost as many
parents alone as there are stars out
on these sharp, moonless nights – in fact, when
I look up, to whatever point in
the sky, I know I'll face a dozen
able to pierce through me, hazy or
bright, each with a dozen bereavements –
you'll find the ache is a thing you can't
do without either, in some queer way...
But here I am, talking as if I'm
antique, instead of being quite a
youngster in the city, not all that
much older or wiser than your small
brother Helderr, whose first world this
is! – and who, if I know anything,

has woken up howling for my milk
by this time! You stay here, Jeserac;
come home to us when you feel ready,
or hungry!

Pomegranate

Each year more clearly you can see her dark flowers wither
to the sick light, or crush to our tighter embrace,
as she picks up her bag and her coat, drifts out to face
the statutory six-months with her mother.

She turns to my heart's cog; rounded, no longer the child
the courts shared between us, as a pomegranate cleft:
small need any more for the fury who would have left
me nothing...though God knows I have never reviled

her. 'Be good to her,' I say, this morning; 'give her
my – ' (I cannot finish). 'And – forget me while you're there.'
'You *both* say that!' She flicks her eyes...'Father, *must* I go?'

My green shoot, Kore, dawdles now at the brightening river's
ferry – waves once – head bent, March uncabling her hair –
then shoulders her bag, full of books I'll expect her to know.

Cygnus A

Removing hairgrips, nail-varnish, pensively brushing
Black hair down to the black
Bra, scattering a thick perfume on the night,
You've time to read me pointed texts
From the Gideons' Bible propped by the red-stained kleenex
Till I must shut my eyes tight
While you slip
Off (still that ludicrous reserve)
Your diaphanous half-slip.

But I prefer to gaze over the dark rooftops
And talk to you over my shoulder.
Somewhere out there, love, near-neighbour Rigel
Winks its white Chaucerian light
From Orion's heel; taking its petty flight
From the peaks of the Eagle
Burning through
Hitler, by Deneb and Altair,
Falls Vega's vulturous blue;

Cambering Perseus covers half the sky,
His spring from the weeping, huddled sisters,
To see if he can reach Andromeda
Before the formless monster lands –
Cassiopeia stretches out her hands;
And out there too's the glare
Of yellow Capella
And red, bull-eyed Aldebaran.
Yet since, sweet, all my stellar

Friends are in fact outshone and liquidated
By the sun streaming from the green shade
Suspended on this window over flickers of you,
I let myself go on and on
Past Deneb, into the dark breast of the Swan
Where only the radio-
Telescope,
Picking up its grating noises
Has any real hope

Of finding out that such a thing exists –
To a celestial catastrophe
Greater than most at various times enacted
In this Trust House – a cataclysm
Unforeseeable by their worst pessimism
– To two galaxies attracted
Into each other
At a slow thousand miles a second
Transformed to a smother

Which astronomers cannot untangle; Cygnus A.
...So girlish, now that your hollow mouth
has shed its lipstick flavour, you hold my hand
Preventively, I kiss black hair,
Your eyes shut tight in pseudo-tragic prayer,
Your weekend penates and
My cupidon
Clutter the bedside-table beside
The white text of St John.

What must it be to have been born inside
Such a fantastic complication –
To pull aside a Cygnian tryst-house curtain
And watch the overwhelming merge
As whistling suns and planets all converge!
For a moment to feel uncertain
If one's discrete
Galaxy will ever emerge
With all its stars complete,

But *only* for a moment – the chances are
That not two single stars will get
Too entangled, as the run-through takes its course
In the next millenium; no glacial
Fate is ready, sweet, to quench an outer-spatial
Swan-light, though scores
Of spheres sail by
Each second – blues, golds and reds
In a greased, fabulous sky.

We're sure to see two 'silver plates' unpair
Round the Year of our Lord 90,000 –
Though, really, five hundred million years ago
These 'lovers' fled away, despite
Curiosity at Jodrell Bank tonight;
No doubt by this time snow
Has covered over
Many a planet, and Judgement-Day
Has heard the excuse of lovers:

'But that was in another galaxy,
And besides, the star is dead!'
While on live red-dwarfs, other will see St John
Shine in your eyes, an aeon hence,
Recording, with their brilliant instruments,
That the red-shift heaven's undergone
So shyly, doesn't veil
Completely the Magellanic Cloud,
Though all the space-trips fail.

Requiem for Aberfan

*On 21 October 1966, in the Welsh coal-mining village of Aberfan,
Tip number 7, containing waste or slurry from the mine, slipped
and overwhelmed Pantglas Junior School. Twenty-eight adults
and 116 children were killed: a generation.*

I.

Magnates whose sweated legions crucified
The valleys, washed their soft white hands, although
The children died before they died.

Brethren who rode their God in on the tide
Of weeping, hawk this good comfort, that we owe
Our deaths to One on green hill crucified.

The child whose dream, the child whose drawing tried
To tell somebody that the hill would flow,
Knew that they died before they died.

Workmen who chose and staked this mountainside,
Their ankles lush with streams, a school below,
Learn on what green hill they were crucified.

Sleepers who from their sheets saw the coal slide
And bury, seven nights before it happened, know
The children died before they died.

Mothers, whose off-to-death sharp voices denied
Fevers and fancies, following at each cock-crow
The road they drove them to be crucified,

Die on the ninth-hour before they died.

II.

There was no keeping out, that day, or keeping in
Either. They set up roadblocks, but you couldn't stop
All Britain pitching in and trying to help.
Or gawp. I stopped one car myself, a whole family,
From the Midlands, 'Is this the place where all those kids
Are buried?' he said. But mostly they wanted to help,
Anything they could do. Which wasn't much.
They didn't have a chance, you see, didn't have a chance...
Yet, you couldn't seem to keep them in. The children.
Not all that lot could. My missus and me, we saw David
A score of times, I suppose, that Friday. He was everywhere!
Running up to the front-door, about to bang it shut,
About to turn the corner. Always *about* to, always three of us,
In the road, in the crowd. Once, I still swear I *did* see him,
In Moy Road, then he vanished. There were the rumours, you see,
Of some being found alive. The whole terrace was like that,
Full of them. No, you couldn't shut them in. It was like
Holes in the slurry you couldn't see. There were
More kids about the place than normal, I'd say.
Funny, it was the same even when I'd found David
In Bethania. Not a mark on him, there wasn't. Like a doll.
We still hoped. It hadn't happened, do you know?

III. *The Father*

The day, you came, I felt her turn from me.
Absence, fullbreasted, coasting at my side,
Straining for different hungers – rightfully.

With no regrets, my pit-black spirit died
And rose like waste through galleries of you.
Cast like a tip, I saw and sang my pride,

The first-born, inexhaustible, the new
Seam, richer, deeper than all Rhondda. A man
Gets born again out of his wife, I knew,

What did it matter that the more you ran
Into your mother's heart, the closer I felt
To an eighth spewed cone out-topping Aberfan?

With no regrets. And yet have I not knelt
Begging God that His curse should overwhelm
Me also, so confirmed was I in guilt

At having willed this on you, in some dream
I had forgotten maybe. When, as the arc–
Lights flickered on the ant-hill, I heard your scream

Rise faintly from a desk, miles deep, the black
Slurry was in myself. Why did we pause?
Now, when the shuddering cage transports us back

To that rise up to hell – untold, we knew –
Always, I hear, faintly, unreachably,
You cry where my own evil fell on you.

IV. *The Brother*

I steal into his room, with my pack of cards,
And play patience under his photo,
Hoping to tempt him.
I get tired of it. It never comes out.

So I go to the mountain, quite a lot.
I remember we had a story once
About how somebody led these children into the mountain,
And there was a lame boy who couldn't go.

Mummy doesn't know, but they have parties in the grave.
Last night, in my sleep, I heard it.
I was in disgrace for telling on them, but I didn't.
Robert called me, Sissy.

The terrace is empty. All summer it's Sunday.
If I showed him my cards, offered to let him win
Only so he would play with me, play,
Would he let me in?

V. *The Doll*

I should have seen her. I might accept it, resign
Myself to having lost her. Not now. You can't
Send your child off to school at nine
O'clock and never see her again. You *can't!*

They wouldn't let me into Bethania, where
They had taken her. I should have fought my way in.
They seemed to think I wouldn't be able to bear
It. The condition she was in.

Because of that, she lives. I put flowers
On her grave like the rest, every day, but she's not there,
Not to me she isn't. It has blue eyes like hers –
Look how they open. To me, she's there,

Shut inside the doll. It was her best doll.
I say Try, darling, try to move
Your arms and legs for me, try. But it's all
That stuff, surrounding, binding. She never moves.

But I can see her struggling. It's such a shame,
All that blackness round them...Sometimes her eyes
Flinch open up at me as though I'll blame
Her for not escaping. As though her eyes

Can see me either! But there is always hope
That one day...And so I keep the room
Exactly as she left it – her books, her skipping-rope,
Her nightclothes. Suppose she woke to a strange room?

People don't like it. Callers say I should free
Myself from the past, that I must forget.
My freedom's here in this room. She grew from me:
Who would remember her if I forgot?

VI. *The Tree*

June. A pallid cloud-drift of sun.
Tree, where a year ago she swung,
Branch and ropes holding the deepening brunt,
Tree, where seven years ago we forked the afterbirth under.

Forked it under, watched it grow. We tried to please,
But there's little enough you could give, to child or tree,
In Aberfan. Watch how coaldust blackens and defeats
In two days the cherry blossom, too late for Easter.

By what trick of its branches' shadow and light
Do I look from the window and see thin limbs flash high?
By what trick of time do I glimpse a torn leaf rise,
Settle? Ah no! a butterfly, a cabbage-white.

VII. *Committal*

Earth trapped our shadows also as we leant
Over the slit-trench.
Bodies saw them die.
Yet when we drifted down the path
– Buoyed up breathless, half-conscious, by communal loss,
As if lifted off our feet by a great crowd
Out of Cardiff Arms Park –
Our bodies stayed behind, our shadows went.

VIII. *The Quickening*

The year turns, to the eve. She lies awake.
Once more the storm comes slanting out of the west.
The younger girl is breathing by her side.
Even so, that night, black drops had slashed the pane.
She flinches; at this hour her child had cried
Out in her sleep, but she has calmed her fears.
She hears the tip upbristling, stormed awake.

Silently, she rises. There are fears
Of rain the spirit in the doll cannot
Express. She crosses the dim passageway,
To comfort it. But it is cold! so trapped!
She bears it downstairs, opens the door, to lay
Her burden in the fury of the storm.
Crying, the storm lacerates her tears.

She mounts. And goes this time into his room.
She melts into his dream of wind and rain.
She hears the loud drops guttering from the eaves
Upon the lonely doll, running the stiff wax,
Releasing limbs beflagged with torn wet leaves,
And as the rain drums on, the quickening breach,
She feels her child's return within her womb.

IX.

The red lights of Tip number 7 gleam through the dusk,
Shutting the stable. It is Christmas. Except in Aberfan.
I stand in the mountainside cemetery, handblowing, cold.
The school is here,
Pantglas School eternally in session.
The master arrived, the names called, and the register collected.
Dyfrig, David, Janette, Kelvyn...
Incorrigible, they are now corrected,
Wilful, in line.

Not requiem, not rest, –
Unrest, mischievousness!
Have them break ranks,
Somewhere, somewhere, a boy set rebellion going!
Dissolve this petrifaction of scripture
Into games, into movement;
Release them to a playground's anarchy.
They have won well their omegas, their black stars,
their death's word-perfect:
They are impatient to say it over, and go.

I would say
Learn, you too-rigid, you too-silencing teacher,
That children can't concentrate
Past bell and alarum, can't concentrate,
As these are doing,
For long.

LOGAN STONE

(1971)

Coma Berenices

Your hair
black, black as the dead, wrong side of the moon,
comet tresses,
if my lips dare probe them, electrically alive as a storm of meteors,
and as mortal to my peace of mind,

elipsed by darkness, the whites of your eyes gleam at me
like the coronae of a binary eclipse,
the cold, still chastity of your thighs where my teeth wander
is the Milky Way, galactic whirlpool and forge
which comes to us as cold, still, chaste light;

the constellations crazy,
their patterns haywire;
in the space of a week
you have flared from nothing into a supernova.

Alphaville

I watch you, glacial in mink,
enter on the arm of your husband,
imperious through the sighs
of your fans, the autographs.
Haughty, you take your seat;
your arm shrinks from his hand;
I whisper into your ear,
I am still crazy for you.
    Mink is as tender as steel
    in alphaville.

He is still crazy for you.
He watches you, late, uncombed,
with lateness on your mind
straight from your doctor's room,
enter the cinema's dark

afternoon, sit straight by him.
Neither yet flickers a sign.
You brush your hair from your eyes.
  Hair is as molten as steel
  in alphaville.

He watches you watching the screen
With never a glance at him.
He watches him loving you,
je t'aime je t'aime je t'aime
he whispers, now as then.
He is still crazy for you.
Your hands touch on the sheet,
like pack-ice, split again.
  Days are as cool as steel
  in alphaville.

Love is a cutting-room, all
images equally true,
I mix them all up in you,
au revoir becomes *je t'aime*
in the crystal at your ear,
as I direct your hand
to stretch for husband, lover;
the camera is crazy for you.
  A film can be cut like steel
  in alphaville.

Your hands in the pit of your back,
steel grapples to eyes of steel;
your breasts on hoardings star;
swiftly you brush your hair;
your husband is crazy for you.
Our son must be fetched from school.
Blinds of the late afternoon
are falling one by one.
  Light opens on the steel
  evening of alphaville.

You are the bathroom-scales'
bland mutability;
the steel tape whips around
your breasts, your waist, your thighs,

inexorably as lovers;
erecting your raised nipples;
it hugs you into despair.
    You ghost into the steel
    slimlines of alphaville.

When, next autumn, next spring,
the houselights go down on this film,
who will be crazy for you,
whispering *je t'aime je t'aime?*
I whisper this in your ear:
stretch out your hand to him,
but remember our mountain-cabin;
preserve it in snow of your tear;
    converse on what is real
    in alphaville.

You are light falling on breasts,
you are a stocking's stretch,
you are the heel on a shoe,
you are a brush through hair,
you are a collar turned up,
you are the leaves you crunch,
you are the wheel of a car,
life is in love with you;
    you are the sad, steel thrill
    that steals through alphaville.

Connemara

So many thousand eyes
– children's, perhaps, or lovers',
blue or grey as the clouds shuffle –
    open in their sleep to me,
    and close again,
    their dream uninterrupted.

    Or the one eye, always.

Kilpeck

On the outside of Kilpeck Church, Herefordshire,
is a celtic gargoyle consisting of head and hands
which are holding open a huge vagina; it is known
locally as the Whore of Kilpeck.

Four calendars rule Kilpeck
    village of church and sheep
between Wales and England past
and present four rhythms
like the church's four winds
The calendar of the sun
    its stormy rising spewing out lambs
    splayfooted by their ewes
The calendar of the saints
    spewing out Love from his tomb
    lamb of god uncertain on his feet
    his shroud like wool tufting the brambles
The calendar of the moon
    ripening the graves' and the castlewalls'
    poison-berries bristling rare cottages' black
    black mountain cats
The calendar of the whore
    sowing the dead with ovarian seeds
    two weeks later dowsing them with blood

This stone cunt stretched wide by stone-hands
is as unfathomably black as the bird-pecked eyes of the sheep-
carcass on the hillside away from the sheltered flock
and twenty yards off her lamb
under the shadow of the crow
who pecks kills pecks
they sow the clean hills with furrows of flesh-stink

The calendars are dissonant
but once in a Great Year
they are in harmony
and then
under the full moon

under the spouting seeds
   of the fullness of the whore's desire
      under the bells of resurrection
        the dead rise
        and couple with each other
        and with the priest and worshippers
        the sons of god come down and couple
        with the daughters of men hair tumbling from
        easter bonnets on the pews and overturned
        gravestones and the pasturing
        hillside a prayer of goodwill
        to all men and peace on earth rises
        from the threshing congregation's congress
        and the stone-cunt's red living lips
        turn upwards and sing
        a hymn of pure love
        in a pure soprano over the
        white mountains

Haiku Sequence

(Nape)
Subtle womanscent
God smelt and approved
even on creation's wrist.

Ghosts. Who taught you
to teach me to kiss
just-behind-the-ear?

Your tenderest inch
any beast's breath could stir
if you did not turn.

With time to spare: Your
pleased turned-away languor
pleases me. Slow thaw.

Your back tenses where
you can't guess where
I can't guess where to land.

Nationalised: rich
seams tapped here
do not make fortunes elsewhere.

Prevented, re-tracing spine,
lips find that blizzards
have buried tracks.

Delighted tongue ravishing
your ear wears like all
males a crude sheath.

(Armpit)
House of Bernarda Alba.
Absorbing, cloistral.
Vulva without doors.

Ear deep-tongued: if
my brain had a Bartholin's Gland
it would be flooded.

Clothed in earrings,
you disengage to strip yourself
submissively naked.

Lazarus-mouth pressed
to this world's black centre
takes his time rising.

Rising, surfacing
with a gasp, I must kiss –
share you with you.

You extract a wet
clinging hair from your mouth:
snake biting its own tail.

His engorgement,
this climbing stretchmark,
unbroken vertical.

Long nails cup and
threaten my manhood:
make me your priest.

I'd live gladly off
your five exudations,
those loaves and fishes.

Ten fingers join hands, dance
in the stifling-hot,
resting arena.

Teeth clamped to my nipple,
you stir
lust out of anger.

Lacquered nail, cold, indulgent,
pierces the anus:
a queen in Soho.

Thighs grip as they lose
the river they will
not wade in twice.

(Interrupt)
Light from receding
galaxies can't keep
pace with itself.

Tell her the stain
on your dress came
from gathering whitecurrants.

I'm abandoned! you whisper-smile,
eyes closed. Face plain,
hair-matted, after love.

Only orifice too
intimate to touch or
kiss: nostrils.

Your middle-finger,
workshy aristocrat,
feels my tongue most.

You, in my pyjama-coat, dropping
spoons: yawning
slut, lust's anagram.

Flecked with red, a white-
packed ashtray invokes
your late guest.

(alba)
Alone
Lying
By your
Anxious flight.

Where the zip caught
your throat, two perfect
fangmarks. Sleep safe tonight.

We look in vain for
those comforting roadsigns
headlights conjure.

Like a motorway's
ill-signed sliproad
somewhere I lost you this time.

Your watching the youth
watching brisk towelled breasts
stiffen, stiffens me.

Eyes jealous even of
the ground's glimpse of flesh-
scything suspenders.

Unreal. In the train
I lift my finger to smell
your faint fingerprint.

Stretchmarks round your
breasts, on your mind,
slowly, slowly fade.

Siamesetwin, newly-stitched,
you jump in sleep.
Your lost self cries out.

On Yeats' tower. The
wind floated your skirt.
Goodbye, wild swan.

(Anniversary)
Joyous laughter. Absurd diners.
Control. Cointreau.
Cunt-roll. Canticle.

(Museum-skeleton with arrow-head)
Ribs and blade: one.
So will love's blade
outlive the flesh it pierced.

Our cigarette afterglows
in car window.
Star-shower from Capricorn.

Seventeen wild strokes.
So much passion needs
your containing scabbard.

Trawl

O fisher-girl,
when the shoal is brought in,
the rich white harvest
leaping and dying on the shore,
and beginning to give off
the smell of decay,
your shoulderblades
pale hungry fins
turn away,
your long, wading thighs
silently weep.

'To Louisa in the Lane'

When Hardy and Louisa in the Lane
(the jump of the hare, says the Kama Sutra)
passed, it mattered not that never again
(the peacock's foot, says the Kama Sutra)

Would he see her white muslin aching by.
(the congress of the deer, says the Kama Sutra)
A moment can dominate memory.
(the line of jewels, says the Kama Sutra)

'Good evening,' he stammered. Their only word.
(the congress of the cat, says the Kama Sutra)
It is doubtful if poor Louisa heard
(the broken cloud, says the Kama Sutra)

As she hurried on, with head downcast.
(the tiger's nail, says the Kama Sutra)
But when Thomas Hardy breathed his last
(a leaf of the lotus, says the Kama Sutra)

After fifty more years of passions and throes,
(the rubbing of the boar, says the Kama Sutra)
The wheelruts and the thorned hedgerows,
(the coral and the jewel, says the Kama Sutra)

And Louisa, long in a Stinsford grave,
(the mounting of the horse, says the Kama Sutra)
Was the last he remembered of human love
(the line of points, says the Kama Sutra).

Lakeside

'*Prove that you love me!*' she said, as a girl will.
'*Anything!*' the boy stammered. '*Anything? Then let me see
you walk the waves.*' He fished for inspiration in her eyes.
And walked. She gave him the spice of her lips, half-mockingly.

'*Prove that you love me! Change the water into wine.*'
She pointed to her pitcher, cracked in the heat of noon.
He lifted an arm. She drank, and hugged her ankles.
Gave him the wine of her tongue, and bit his own.

'*Prove that you love me!*' '*Anything.*' '*I'm hungry now.
Change this dry crust to a feast, and don't be long.*'
There were baskets to spare. She bared her small teeth in pleasure.
Spared him the roes her breasts – then away she sprang.

Hid herself in a rock. Tortured, he seized her.
But she wriggled like a lizard away. '*Prove
that you love me!*' A cripple was passing. '*Heal me him.*'
The cripple walked. For an instant his finger clove

the hill of frankincense, but again she twisted
out of his grasp, her laugh invaded by a gasp of pain.
She stood on the rock, goading, belly thrust forward.
'*Prove that you love me! Die for me,*' she said.

'*Die, and you can have this. Not unless.*' She kilted
her robe, pulled open the sepulchre to show the red
sand-flesh waiting. Speech and colour left his lips.
'*So you* don't *love me!*' She laughed, spat grossly, and fled.

Wandering to the shore, he helped the fishermen
with their nets; but his mind and his blood ran
on the frightening fount of energy that had leapt in him.
She bitched about homelong, blood splashing like menstrual wine

that flowered lemon-trees in her aimless wake;
forgot by dusk the strange shy clumsy boy,
knowing too well the power in her little finger
to stir such deeds, and more, when the devil was in her.

Logan Stone

if it were one
stone   it would not be magical
if it were two stones   the attrition of
rain cutting into its natural weakness too well
it would not be magical if its massif could be set
trembling   neither two nor one for a moment only   say
the logging-point of night-fall it would be magical yet
not miraculous   small worlds may be born of such magic
but that it can go on and on   without ceasing   dazzling
the spectator with immobile motion neither two nor one
neither one nor two doomed and unshakable on its point
of infinity   that is the the miracle   to be so weak
a finger logs it   what constant strength
what force it takes to be a
logan-
stone you and I what cold applied
granite-fire logging on weakness no storm can move us

Penwith

Did flint tools or alone the driving rain
complete its holy paradox: granitic
yet sensitive as the joint of a bone?

Nine maidens petrified for sabbath dancing
or sun-discs crouched in an altar-less ring,
in a misty field the sea's whetstone hones
to a sharp blade; the sun tests it, aslant.

On the humped moor's spine, consumptive miners
turned aside from their plod home to crouch and pass
through the men-an-tol, the ring of granite.

I am the loganstone a cloud can alter,
inert mass trembling on a compass-point;
I am the men-an-tol, the wind's vagina;
I am the circle of stones grouped around grass.

Botallack

Needles flake off into the blue air. Listen.
In the August silence, on the bare cliff-path, you can fling
a stone and it will not break the silence, but you can hear
the wedges and drills of erosion hammering
in a silence that is uproar, beneath the wrecking Brissons.

The sea might ring to a finger today. Bone-china.
Without the drama of weathers, no flowers or trees
to mask time with recurrence, time's raw nerve
shows through here like an outcrop of tin. A peace
that is the acceptance of defeat reigns. Miners

50

trekked this vertical, nerves tempered granite;
at their head, candles – defeat – disaster – dowsed,
to stride out under the sea as courageous,
poor in all but tall tales the ocean housed,
as their methodist Christ walked out upon it.

Botallack locks against too strong a force;
blue-framed, nettled engine-house, cliff-set. The logan stone
of me is here. Bal-maidens spalling ore
for bread feared not the plunge. Why should I alone
stride ahead of the flood, on a white sea-horse?

Down in those spirit-heights, if the guttering
candles failed, kind-
ly light amidst the encircling gloom, one man
guided them unfailingly through blackwaters. He was blind.
In the country of the blind, that man was king.

The Shaft

A few tin-mines in Cornwall are being re-opened by international combines. The shaft in the poem is one and many, like the persona: who is variously a foreign mining-engineer, myself, my father, dead miners related to me.

Under the trapped sky, turning on itself the wind
whips up concrete. On my office-wall, a diagram
of the old workings; mirror where soft lined graphite
simplifies to a lying order the
shaft. Long ago that face abandoned me.
I give my curt instructions as they wind
the bucket down. It bears a Sunday freight.
Shout to the tourist to keep his elbow in.
His face is that Englishman my tank ran down, cream.
This is Cornwall, or the possibility of tin,

or any of sixteen other god-
forsaken holes. The consortium pays well.
Last year, in Ontario, mica.
The year before, in Alaska, an oil-well.
Next year, when this is working, Africa
and diamonds. Each of those absurd places
grows perhaps an image of myself.
Cunts are the only certain good
shafts. In Chile, Poland, Malay, traces
of the boar, the maze bull, and the wolf.

Only inside my skull do I feel our fall.
'This thing scares the shits out of me, I don't mind tellin'
'ee. I'll be glad when the fucking skip is ready.' Their blunt
purity with words troubles me. I use fuck
to bring myself off in my mistress's cunt.
Opening in half-light. Floodroar drifts up past.
'A million gallons a day and that old shaft's still full.'
My fathers raised through this shaft far more than tin.
My son won't be Cornish. No redwater from my past
drains into my black.

Breast-pocketed under my circus-act overall,
seven brothers, seven miners, stand imploded, photographed;
the youngest, in petticoats between the double-stars:
my father. Many times they threaded this shaft.
Their deaths permit them here the illusion of futures.
But nothing has happened since.
The explosion has happened that sent them all
hurtling apart, to Lima, Hollywood, Jo'burg, Butte City,
deaths; but face my heart, an achievement, a unity.
One great-aunt, full of her marginal existence,

faces aside from the camera. One son still
remained unborn. My reason for being. Dead at eighteen. My grand-
mother's letter to America, on flake-thin
paper. 'I was down last Saturday to Donald's grave
took down all the nice roses and some lilies and
when I realised that was all I could ever do
for him I thought I could cry until
there were no more tears to shed I stayed
there some time and talked to him there was not a soul in
the churchyard and I wondered how I could live through

but I got home had a bad headache...' Our summerplace apart;
a modernised tin-streamer's cottage, said the brochure.
Transistor, black stockings, books, ghosts spill from your case.
Shaver, contraceptives, books, ghosts spill from my case.
Clear water from the shower
runs over our play as from some long dead heart.
All night I dream of casualties
unknown to your quiet Saxon breath.
The living cells are underneath
the dead cells of the skin I kiss.

> Acts of love
> impel you
> to move
> by rote
> on again
> and down.
> By rite
> the next
> presses you
> footflexed

onto the sollar
    and off again
    gripping
    the man-
    engine-rod

These are moments of the chances
of exit: water
or breeze hurrying across
the line of shaft
like a sudden smell
blazing back childhood
or white arm across my body
or that girl in the Hollywood rosebowl float that smiled.
Such moments may be found years later
gorse-covered holes in the hillside
by tourists.

Why did I come home? To comfort
mother, Donald dead. To reknit the faulted rock
marrying Amy. A wife in a million. She understood
and shielded me from the tongues' pitiless stamps. We
went everywhere in a threesome. That adit ended
as though by a sign the day May bled
from her playing-up womb. She raised her skirt,
red flow like her suspenders, frank with shock.
Blood stained the picnic-cloth. I stood
astonished. Gave her my handkerchief and walked away.

It widens. We pull the skip door back
to strike the echo. It is the mine's
chapel. Tenors ring out Deep Harmony. They exalt
the Lord of the bal. Backs straighten, mouths crack white. I exult
in my voice, as its bass catches and matches lower
the echo, tin under copper again, terrific bronze,
defiant
joy unifies the smutched pit-head flower
and the giant
fins brushing 8 level. This cuts the dark back.

Perhaps somewhere
also, a wife, a son. Also perhaps
a mistress. Certainly photos of two women
and a boy share my desk with fool's gold. I am vague.
Take home from the pub some little Cornish whore,
strip tights, pants, go into that curious hole.
I am a skilled opener of mines. Then
a tiny tremor as of acute fatigue
and the total infalling collapse.
Something lay still, or moaned, lay still. I stood whole

and exonerated, lit a cigarette. Certain women
trouble me with headache as I check each steel strand.
A small inspection crew down. Hangovers man
the head. This morning I left my flask behind
and had to go back. It is an ill omen.
Now that face: I put it on a charge; it stares
at me in dumb insolence. The whole
mixed-racial crew will back it to a man
against me. That face is out of control.
Not even the threat of execution stirs

any sign of feeling. It holds me to it.
I'll break. I am nothing but this drilling head
I drink to clear. A mineral survey lies
spread out and optimistic. They failed to exploit
so many difficult lodes. Hastily they left;
this jacket we found in a dry stope
a mile from the main shaft.
Yet when my dynamiter lays
fresh face bare, they've raised the best. Hope
dwindles. Deep laughter trickles up through the head.

Every suck of air
mallets deeper dust's
drills. Though eight mouths cry for food
they will put me out to graze,
climb scaffolds, carry the hod, reduced
to that height. Why drink foul water through teeth
clenched to keep out the maggot death?
Few clear forty. And age is a tragedy, my sonnies.
My way is clear, my account square.
What if I step back into air?

Blind engine-house. Botallack's
blank eyes, great hammered face and ruined phallic
stack, released from sight
to a boy's outsight
I see the sublimity
of what is called failure. Rubbed
away between sea and granite, robbed
of all features, a dry
for the salt drab wind.
Love is the only sense that survives, honed.

Again the bladder stings. Penis half-hard,
agony soon. The spunk dies, they say. Day and night
hospital/operation flashes like a traffic-light.
With my bare hands I could tear the props down,
but I shall come out feet first. My son
won't have to work hard, thank God. I see him feel
his fiancée in the back pew. She's nice legs. He'll reason
a way to stay home. Will hear the choir swell
the last hymn, scaring down his hard-
on, across the field. All is nearly gathered in.

I drilled two points of light in a vertical stope.
My son remains. He is my exit, my hope.
Over supper tell them Jimmy Hardhead's latest:
Jimmy's boots were taking water, so I said to him, Why don't you get
a new pair of boots, Jimmy? Ess, he said, I believe I will. He came
hobbling to work today, crippled up. He'd bought two sizes too small.
Well, no wet feet today, Jimmy? I said. No, he said, no room for no
bleddy water in there.
I start the laugh myself, it cracks like a rockslide.
The pit-head laughs at their laughter at my laughter.
Letting some light rise.

How could I know,
not knowing he was ill,
telling him that nurse's anecdote,
how the unshaven shaver of the wards
had earmarked the florins on a brow,
'then in the morning the bugger hupped and revived!'
I hear his laughter jet.
Did it help to kill?

I remember almost his last words:
'I caught his eye this morning on me.' He revived,

or seemed to, toward dawn. We saw later
it was the way a lift first rises a shade
to settle into its groove, no more than that.
How imperceptible, though, that final fall.
Some time after the last insucking cough
we had to presume he had reached a kind of level
no one had passed before. My mother made
me look away, praying. I noticed later that
his laundered pyjamas held his handkerchief,
not to be signed for, wringing with living water.

          The child I willed
          when my cries
          were to
          that hole
          will hear
          a shade
          whisper
          over me too
          'Donald',
          smell lilies
and roses.

It is good that I can't look up or down.
How else could I travel? Yet still I shake.
One dank patch, cement-pipe, air-pipe, water-pipe, illumined
by their headlamps. There is too much pressing sweat.
They are my father, I love them, I cannot speak.
I crave death in a cigarette.
I would give the words I have mined
to exchange one word with them
on some casual theme.
I mine and go down.

My arm jammed against the bucket's lip
and my long terror of falling comes home to roost
where deep in my molecules this precipitous face is
pumping familiar adrenalin. The wheal is mine.
White teeth, white eyes, my vertical faces

step in time onto the man-engine-
rod, are carried down, step back, the slight shudder
increasing; or they swarm the ladder,
their young sons on their backs; or in the skip
their lives briefly at rest.

A boy, I dropped a stone into this shaft,
and still I wait for it to strike old
bones, rust, water. The bucket lurches
and I don't know if I have come far or at all.
But this is the drowned legend, poverty without mineral,
wrecks, the hundred engulfed churches
and chapels, all the sea-horses killed
but mine. Not as I went through my mother's shaft
I am alone.
The square of one is one.

LOVE AND OTHER DEATHS
(1975)

Nurses

Longshoremen

What strange cargoes

what crude-packed cargoes they load or unload
with a nonchalant expertise
as though saying
there is more
there is always more

the owners calm down
shakily join in the banter
it is not life or death

whatever sent forth
white meat
delicate jewelled instruments
there is meat enough in their own larders
watches on their own wrists
held out and sustaining
the otherways-gripped load so steadily

they appear to know to the split-second
when the scarcely moving hulk
has passed in hazy water
the line of indisputable demarcation

it is good
it is all good

on the waterfront
        to smoke the good cigarette

on the water
                to be so still

Cecie

The evening that you died was the first I could not
Overhear you bed-down with your 'dear Nellie':
No farting and whispering. The house lay cursed
Not with one death only: with its own.
Who, you asked in my head, will lace my brother's
Shoes up in the morning, empty the chamberpots
And dress my sister? There was no reply.
I heard you struggle to sit up in the coffin.
You'd have worked all night and worked off that deep hurt.

Dear aunt, if Christ had come, as well he might, to you,
You'd have scrubbed his feet with good soapy water
Left from Monday's wash, pocketed a few
Fresh loaves and fishes for your poor sister;
Burnt your hand on the boiler, muttered, 'That's nothin',
Run out, lisle stocking flapping, to dig the garden.

You demand – clucking at the grave in such a state,
From our habit of taking you for granted – shears,
Scrubbing-brush, water, not for your sake but hers
You lie beside again. An image of you: triangle:
Lawn, mower and you (no taller than it)
Leaning a force three times your fleshless weight.
70, your death shocked us like a child's.

In all but stoicism you *were* a child.
Rampaging through the village you never left,
Blackberry-faced, hot pasties in your apron,
Scuttling, chuckling. No breasts to hold or suck at.

You had no life. No lovers that I know of.
Yet we all loved you. You were filled with love
No one repaid. Death can't be a still
Nor a cobwebbed house any longer, full of your labour,
Farting, scurrying. You have no death.
So much living is living still.

The Journey

Mother, hear the wind keening over the Goss Moor,
Tregeagle's sighs, emptying the bottomless Dozmare
Pool. Seeing the world again begins to bore
You. You rub seized joints. I ask you how you are
And the wind fails to force the car
Off the A30. Yes, it is good of me to drive so far,

For one almost as old and bald as Dozmare,
Her life, apart from me, featureless as Goss Moor.
I compute how far
We have to go: seven hours. She who bore
Me is pressed, small, while the decimal nines are
Flickering into noughts, back into the car,

As I was, waiting. I ask how you are;
Must I wind down the window a shade, raise the car-
Heater? It is wrinkled Tregeagle emptying the Dozmare
Pool in you, discomfort, pain, that never fall far
Before rising to the same level. Your harpings bore
Me like this incessant wind over the Goss Moor.

And I cannot look sideways in the car,
It is too painful to see how shrunken you are,
Tacitly, since last the Goss Moor
Shot past us, and hidden Dozmare;
Three thousand miles on the gauge since I came so far
To fetch you. That January day you bore

Me, did the journey feel so far?
Image of starry countdowns that move and bore
Us, I dice with the petrol countdown, see if the car
Will reach the next pump, past Bodmin Moor.
You rest trustful in my omniscience. Old Dozmare
Mother, what strange things and what strangers we are.

I know these three weeks you will bore
Me. I don't read your letters when you are far
Away, those cheerful comforting lies. So; till you are
Dead, as something wants, and, dead, I drive this car
Or the next, for the last time up through the moor
That rose when Dozmare was sea, and sees the end of Dozmare.

I help you struggle from the car, to a moorstone. You bore
Your own small Dozmare in thin soil. For we are water and moor,
And far journeyers together. Whatever else we are.

Reticent

How they loved understatement!
'Goin' a' drop rain, are us?' – the sky
an enraged bladder. 'He've had a drop to drink.'
'I dear like bit ride' – those grotesque tea-treat safaris
to Weston-super-Mare or Timbuctoo,
with a break for drop tea and a brisk turn
round the amazement-arcades before starting back.
'Nice few taties this year, 'n?' 'Nice bit o' meat, plenty
for all of us.' 'He've got a shillin' in his purse'
– John Jago with his Johannesburg gold-shares.
'Are you goin' to kiss me? 'Cause you're goin' away
for a few minutes' – I to my Oxford term.
It expressed their landscape;
deep labyrinths under the shafted bracken.

Now a drop of rain drums on a good few graves.
Plenty enough for me.
Some with not even a jampot to catch it.
When I've had a drop to drink
I can bear my mother's lonely, painful descent;
'You're not looking too bad.'
Cursed with the style, I felt embarrassed to
bend and kiss my father's tortured face,
he 'no better' behind the corner screen,
he going away for a few minutes.
Liking bit ride, I drive 200 miles
to glance at my watch till it's time to go again.
Without exaggeration the landscape weeps.
I've got a shilling but I can't spend it.

Rubble

I sit in my mother's cramped bedsit,
on edge in body and spirit.
The light too bright for her eyes.
The radio too loud for her ears.
The low fire too hot for her
seized limbs appalling me.

Yet she wants to live.
Yet to rejoin her husband.
To win, lose, tie, go on running.

Almost it is a quarter to nine
when I can jump up, heat
her milk and water, kettle
for her bottle, pull out the commode,
compel myself to kiss her, and go.

She is a fledgling
broken on the road
I want to be out of sight of.
But alive, or the world will fold.

It is as though the black hole
drawing her into itself
is conditioning my love
to require absence. She knows

it. She is content. There is
a queer radiance in the space
between us which my eyes
avoid occupying: the radium
Madame Curie found, when desolate
she returned at night to the empty table.

Poem of the Midway

Where shall we meet, Marina
Tsvetayeva? Have you any
suggestions for our rendezvous?
And in what year?
I shall clutch a photo of you, .

but what of the breath
rising and falling under your
coat, your flush, your rumpled
hair? (You'll run from the station.)
What will you wear?

Somewhere midway. Not in your own
city, Moscow. They stole that
from you. Perhaps in Prague,
the embankment, or the café
full of whores and tears
where your love left you –
yes? (I am jealous.)

Somewhere midway. Or I
will come further, let's say 1950
(aren't lovers prone to
pathetic rushed decisions!) ten
years beyond your death, twenty
behind me now. And not
any street that is likely to
rob me of your whole
joy: you will kiss

more beautifully than any,
and I will love you so fiercely
the wild nerves of your poems
will translate straight into my tongue.
Dress for me with the tremulous
awarenesses of the stripped.
(My hand trembles, shaving.)

Our small talk through our night
together! (We won't sleep.)
I know from your poetry
what you think of God, love,
and your life – that suburb
of a town you're exiled from,
but I want to know your tastes
in wine, clothes, films.

Where shall we meet, Marina
Tsvetayeva? Anywhere in Europe
and our century will be dark
enough for our assignation,
and your poems I'll come holding
will give us enough light
to talk by, across a table.
How cool your hand is.

Kore

Your mouth
is music heard
faintly outside the house
of a maestro

your love
is not in cries or spasms
but in the particular curve
and fluttering movement
of your unseen arms

Marriage of Venice to the Sea on Ascension Day

Gaspara Stampa (1523-54) wrote her most intense love-sonnets not long before her death, and in the year of Titian's Danaë and the Golden Shower. *One of the sonnets, which lament her lover's desertion, concludes: 'He in whom I find new perfections, As a trained eye finds out new stars.'*

1

Gaspara Stampa on the Bridge of Sighs.
No feeling surfaces to her cold form
That she is tortured by this meeting-place.
A hand, bloodied by nails, has drawn across

Light a rich scumble of unclearable cloud,
A golden excrement. Her god had come,
Walked on her waters; rises, vanishes.
His gold ring plunges through immensities

Into the canal whose hymen breaks.
She is left by what she is left with: love.
The artist breaks and re-sets, breaks and re-sets,
Shivering like a chain of gondolas;

From his corruption new perfections rising
To her, as a trained eye finds out new stars.

2

Till choice and chosen are suggested there,
The artist breaks, re-sets, breaks and re-sets
Her arm bent on the linen, troubling his sleep.
In excremental gold the god has come.

Now it is finished save the masterstrokes.
His gold ring plunges through immensities;
With his fingers only he perfects
The hand between her thighs, and draws across

Her upturned gaze the limits of creation.
The hymen is broken and the waters break,
The god-child breasts the breakers. He cleans his hands,

And his trained eye already finds new stars.
He turns the imperfect canvas to the wall,
Where she will find, in darkness now, his love.

3

The Bridge of Teats receives the water-Christ's
Benediction. Greeting the holy form,
In the film of sweat that glistens on her breasts
Each whore has traced with scarlet nail a cross.

Jesus the sun amidst white neophytes.
In golden vesture their God has come,
His gaze fixed high above San Marco's lion
As a god's vision might find out new stars.

The crowds fall to their knees. San Marco booms.
He walks the waters, rises, vanishes.
They jostle, embrace. They have seen the groom's
Gold ring flying through immensities.

The Doge puts out to sea. Gold fetors rising
Light a rich scumble of reflective cloud.

4

The lion interrupts with wilder, blue
Light the rich scumble of reflective cloud.
It is high afternoon of the young summer.
Stone walks the waters, water springs from stone.

All delight seems streaming into the city,
To celebrate a tremulous meeting-place.
Action and passion, energy and peace;
Ancient fountains free a hardening form.

Into a glazed lagoon a whore has pissed
A golden excrement. No god has come
With greater ecstasy than her affected

Shivers. Lying back in the gondola,
She takes by chance the image of Danaë,
Warm flesh-tones leaning on a bridge of sighs.

5

They rest, on the Adriatic's bluest skin,
To celebrate a tremulous meeting-place.
The cardinal prays that marriage make them dearer
As a trained eye finds out new stars.

Trumpets. The Doge opens the silver casket.
The hymen is broken and the water breaks.
Under the resettled iconostasis
A gold ring plunges through immensities.

The Doge is moved. He is that mirage
Which walks the waters, rises, vanishes.
Flambeaux flame on the galleys, augment with hymen-
Light the burnt scumble of reflective cloud

Which in the choppier waters, as dusk settles,
An artist breaks, re-sets; breaks, re-sets.

6

He must, must break his custom. Turns to him
The smiling nude. Draws a sharp breath; and sighs:
Seeing the universe concentrated where
A warm canal, beneath the illusioned form,

Secretes the shower her servant cannot catch,
And comes, with ripples like a gondola's.
Yet he, the maker's maker, cannot lie
To consummate a tremulous meeting-place,

Until reality and shadows mix
And into paint his blood is drawn across.
His old hand trembles, touches her shadowy hollow

From whose miasma new perfections rise,
As though his finger could slide in with god.
His gold ring plunges through immensities.

7

The Doge is crying. He has seen his death
Touching his life, a lovers' meeting-place,
In Titian's portrait. He smiled and gave the gold,
But shuddered. Now the chain of gondolas

Turns from the Grand Canal into his death.
The hymen is broken and the waters break.
His gondolier negotiates a canal
Unexpected, tight, like the cleft cut by love

In time's unyielding stone embattlements.
From its miasma new perfections rise
Solacing his heart. A phantom leans.
Her hand, dyked by its blood, is drawing a cross

Over her heart's decision of solitude,
As a trained eye finds out new stars.

8

A high wind blows in salt to her cloaked face.
Night's hymen's broken, her reflection breaks
Under her. A cannon's boom. Carnival shouts.
The rising flood becomes the meeting-place

Of fireflies and contagion. From her despair,
A phrase. Out of it new perfections rise.
A sonnet begins to live. From the wide sea,
Images, like the Doge's gondolas,

Negotiate into lagoons, canals.
The whole world's waters move through a cold form.
Most flows away again. Poetry's stone

Walks on the waters, rises, vanishes.
Even the flowing out she gathers in,
Building out of all loss a Venice, love.

Poem in a Strange Language

Starlings, the burnable stages of stars,
Fall back to earth, lightly. And stars,
Propulsars of angels, die in a swift burn.
And half the angels have fallen below the horizon.

And, falling like alpha particles,
Re-charge the drowned woman
Floating in the bitter lake,
Her hair gold as their blood, her face amazed.

She is Lot's wife, her naked body
Sustained by the salt she has loosened from,
And as her eyes open, grain
Turns green-golden on the black earth of Sodom.

I enter your poem, Mandelstam, yours, Anna
Akhmatova, as I enter my love –
Without understanding anything
Except its beauty and law.

And the way its cloud of small
Movements lifts lightly the fruit
Of a painful harvest and moves
With singing vowels away from death.

Friday Evening

You are on the train crawling across country towards me.
I am in the car driving to a half-way station.
You are switching on the overhead reading-light.
I am switching on the car sidelights.
You are losing yourself in a book.
I am losing myself in a poem.
I know this road like the palm of your hand.

To give up is as desperate as to go on.
You lean your head on the glass, speckling with rain like sperm.
I switch on the wipers.
Dusk deepens.
The station will always be there to meet us,
Unable to go even when the last train is in,
Even when the sun flickers low, a waiting-room fire.

Nightride

Clairvoyants are hurling in thousands
their tiny bodies against our windscreen.

We have headaches; I switch on
the wipers, splash up some water.

Catlights hypnotise my headlights
round hairpin bends and adjustments.

Clairvoyants are hurling in thousands
their tiny bodies against our windscreen

and somewhere beyond their amazing splats
against 70 mph reinforced glass,

behind our car,
the small gnats and flies wing on
where their deaths have not yet hit them.

Surgery

She is the doctor of verities.

She says to the woman, You must leave him who is your love
and your life, or you will not live.
Here is valium.
It will take you on a train journey
but it will lead only to a station
late at night, that knows only two directions,
the asylum, and a street without addresses.

She says to the man, You must leave her you do not love
even though love says you cannot.
Here is librium.
It will take you on a plane-flight,
but at its grounding your love and your love
will arrive together like cases on the revolving track,
both full of almost identical woman's things,
one with so many articles of you, and so many children's,
and you must pick up one. It is impossible any more
to pick up both. One must go on revolving
and you must walk away.
And she writes, for the woman and for the man,
separately,
prescriptions in a language
she herself hardly begins to know.

Something to carry her into the terrible valley.
Something to carry him into his terrible liberation.

She does not know what kind of whole
she is asking them to fall into.
She trembles.
Her own issue of blood
wanting to touch some god's garment.

You Are on Some Road

The evening star
trembling in blue light

The red star
breaking through the dusk
like acetylene

The Orion stars
blossoming
like desert flowers

Even the Pleiads
sharply visible
like children in white
on a dark street

Tribes of stars
never seen before
drumming beyond the drift
of the Coal Sack

You are on some road

FROM Sonoran Poems

I descend I enter you
a diplomat sick of negotiations
choosing to be hijacked
by a blue stewardess
with a gun instead of champagne

in the midst of a ghost town
in the midst of a desert
to rest
to forget time and the six
directions to be forgotten

Like a kachina-mask
you wear your beauty like a kachina-mask
      your beauty

the minute you are gone
   desert rain
      red
      mariposa lilies
      astonished
      mariposa lilies

From desert scrub the lord's candles glimmer
a wind shivers and I am changed

without knowing it yet
without holding it yet
mistaking it for joy

I become good
I become loyal to myself

moment by moment
new stars made

O Mother of Tonantsin
O Our Lady of Guadeloupe

The bulb-light flickers
figures are there searching
combing the ghost-town

You stand with blue lips
back to the door
alien and fanatic
covering me

But how can love recede
but how can love recede
those slit domes
through which the night keeps pouring

It is my kachina-mask
it is my kachina-mask
instead of patched jeans
you come to me dressed
as the traditional spy
and seducer quelling your nature
it is my birthday you say

long black gloves
garterbelt and stockings
tense as a strung bow

I fuck it as I pretend
it is you I fuck
it is the fetish I fuck
it is the god

the mountain around which
everything moves it is here
and here and here
in these fulcra of greatest anguish

I adore the oppugnant stresses
agent and double agent and triple agent

wearing my kachina-mask
I will betray anything
wearing my kachina-mask

You
the song
bring a smile to my lips
I cannot silence

Muse you are dead
why do you walk along my dreams
my dry veins
hunting your murdered children
and wailing and scratching huge rents
in the backs of lost travellers
like the ghost-woman of the sandflats of the Santa Cruz

I am tired of faces
that shine next to me as close
as a filling station the other side a motorway
softly shining
at night

Let the downpour be stored

My soul is very lonely
blind he has touched your face
he sends me to be a go-between
to beg you to come

bring a flower of the saguaro cactus
to cure my friend

The Indian cemetery at Xan Xavier
square and facing east
their white and nameless crosses

your hand gently enchaining me
and your eyes with love releasing me
it is not of death I think
on this happy day
but as if the whole universe moves towards the east

THE HONEYMOON VOYAGE

(1978)

Diary of a Myth-Boy

Something called Death came today. Witch-
doctor has this big dream,
tells him three canoes sailing down-
stream, Immortal Spirit
in third one. So he lines us all up.
Sure enough, about noon,
canoe comes, full of rotten fruit.
That's Death, says the witch-doctor. White
man comes sailing down in
second canoe, and our stupid
sod of a witch-doctor
wades out and embraces him! Down
comes Immortal Spirit in third
canoe, waving his arms
shouting, That's Death, you fool, can't you
even count up to three?
He just stood, scratching his head and
grinning, he's not all there...

Grandmother comes to me in the
night, squats on my face and
farts. If you ask me she's crazy.
This afternoon sharpened
my arrow-heads...

                    Followed mother
when she went out gathering
palms to make my penis-sheath. Saw,
as she climbed to the top,
my first cunt, rich as a date. Raped
her. Told grandmother. She
said, You're a big boy now, but watch
out for your father. If he
sends you to the region of souls,
take a hummingbird with
you. Crazier and crazier...

Sick all morning. Could this
be pregnancy, or grandmother's
farts? My father in a

terrible temper, tells me to
set out tomorrow for
the region of souls, to fetch a
dance-rattle. Sure thing my
mother's ratted on me, the cow...

Grandmother's dead. When she
came last night I stuck an arrow
up her arse. Her guts fell
out. God, she was rotten. No more
entries for a few days.
Lots to write about, I expect,
when I come back...

                    Granny
was right about the hummingbird.
Dance-rattle hung from a
cord, hummingbird's beak cut it. It
splashed into the river,
alerted the souls who fired their
arrows in. If I'd been
there I wouldn't be writing this.
Dance-rattle floated to
me. Grandmother wise woman. When
I got home, mother and
sister sick, father away hunting
– I'd like to have seen that
bastard's face. No food cooked...

Mother and sister dead, with most
of the other women.
Sister goes to my hut to fetch
dead fish, takes granny's guts
instead. Stupid bitch! It's poison
of course. Everyone who
ate it, died. They call it Disease.
Saves me the bother of
killing mother for tale-telling...

No girls left. We boys muck
about among ourselves. We're all
pregnant but can't bear kids.
It's no fun cooking and cleaning,
and with fat bellies too.
What a life!...

Got my revenge on
father today. Put on
antlers, met him out hunting, speared
him. Flung him in the lake.
Spirits must have got him, his lungs
floated up...

Saw this girl,
up a tree, the first for bloody
months. Chatted her up, it
turned out she didn't like fish. I
tried to climb the trunk but
my erection got in the way,
came all over it and
gave up. A crowd of the other
lads came at her through the
treetops, raped her, then cut her up
into little pieces.
Which, as they slid down the trunk, met
my sperm and of course turned
into girls. I got a thick slice
of rump and my girl's well
stacked. Some of them are skin and bone...

God it's a boring life,
no tribes to fight with, all killed off
by Disease (grandmother
started something there), my
fat wife a pain in the arse. A
white anthropologist
who's turned up here's been telling me
about life with his folk.
It sounds really exciting. I'm
going to pack a few
pearls and things tonight, slip this
diary under the
anthropologist's tent-flap and
sneak away up river...

(Acknowledgments to tribal myths of Central Brazil)

Whale

A whale lay cast up on the island's shore
  in the shallow water of the outgoing tide.
    He struggled to fill his lungs,
    he grew acquainted with weight.

And the people came and said, Kill it, it is food.
And the witch-doctor said, It is sacred, it must not be harmed.
And a girl came and with an empty coconut-shell
  scooped the seawater and let it run over the whale's blue bulk.

A small desperate eye showing white all round
  the dark iris. The great head flattened against
    sand as a face pressed against glass.

And a white man came and said, If all the people
  push we can float it off on the next tide.
And the witch-doctor said, It is taboo, it must not be touched.

And the people drifted away.
And the white man cursed and ran off to the next village for help.

And the girl stayed.
She stayed as the tide went out.
The whale's breath came in harsh spasms.
Its skin was darkening in the sun.
The girl got children to form a chain
of coconut-shells filled with fresh water
that she poured over his skin.

The whale's eye seemed calmer.

With the high tide the white man came back.
As the whale felt sea reach to his eye he reared
on fins and tail flukes, his spine arced
and he slapped it all down together, a great leap
into the same inert sand.
His eye rolled

in panic as again he lifted and crashed down,
   exhausted, and again lifted and crashed down,
      and again, and again.

The white man couldn't bear his agony and strode away,
   as the tide receded.
He paced and paced the island and cursed God.

Now the whale didn't move.
The girl stroked his head
and as the moon came up
she sang to him
of friends long dead and children grown and gone,
sang like a mother to the whale,

and sang of unrequited love.

And later in the night
   when his breaths had almost lost touch
      she leant her shoulder against his cheek

and told him stories, with many details,
of the mud-skipping fish that lived
   in the mangroves on the lagoon.

Her voice
and its coaxing pauses
was as if fins
were bearing him up to the surface of the ocean
to breathe and see,
as with a clot of blood falling on her brow
the whale passed dear from the body of his death.

(After an incident in Lyall Watson's Gifts of Unknown Things*)*

84

A Cornish Graveyard at Keweenaw
(North Michigan)

Harriet Uren, 100, eighty years from Penzance,
Died with the scent of saffron in the cloam.
Daughter and great-grandmother, felt death enter
Like the slow dark voyage down the home coast.
Plymouth was strange, Fowey less; she could not weep
Though grown men wept, as hymn on hymn unrolled
The Lizard, flashing. Then the Mount, the light,
Only a miner's daughter could have seen,
Drawing away as she drew nearer home.

Turned then, bride to groom, and went below.
Undressed in the dense dark, too shy to breathe.
Surrendered to what might come, her eyes chatoyant,
Rocked in fusions
Of gain and loss and that sustaining rise.
Praying only this night what may suffice,
She slept. Couples embrace, weep, talk,
Or sleep. On deck, the Scillies past, the seethe
Of brotherly harmony grows coarse and buoyant.

And here intuited their second life.
That granite outcrop grew them, this grew with them.
Cherished rock more than they cherished flesh, drilled,
Blasted it, as they went, sang as they went.
Stillness in this boomed peninsular
Unrest. Yet so much, and such dry, Cornish
Wit, together! Such eager harmonies
To such handsome voices keen to pitch a tune!
Praise God for the water's lap, the same horn-thrust.

And all in time who went on to unlock
Nevadan silver, Californian gold,
Great pranksters, wrestlers and evangelists,
Wondered before they died or slept
Which was their home, Cornwall or Keweenaw.
The seams of want and wanderlust
Compelled new shafts of love, but those clairvoyant
And helmet eyes still saw a celtic cross
And window-light, their roots their albatross.

Sumach sighs, and the great lake locks in ice.
You are luminescent with impurities,
Tarnished with fractures, silky with inclusions,
Your winks and laughter ride out circumstance,
You prod each other with ironic fists.
Tin into gold, my sonnies, my alchemists,
You who're quicksilver like New Almadén –
Where now? Impossible you'll stay in baulk,
With that swift talk, in pulses, like your sea.

Decks crammed like troopships, or pared, two
By two, hard-rock miners driving into talc,
Ricepaper clinging to honeymoon silk.
I praise God's ship of death, restorative,
Hiding the bone, healing the lung's scar,
And imagine what Liberty has hushed their dry
Expanding stories awhile, their souls raw,
Their eyes bright, moving west across the spectrum
Of hard rock, giving new land new energy.

Under Carn Brea

Grandmother

In a room with drawn venetian blinds
I was carried to you, and took from your hands
Green grapes. Though your hands and face frightened
Me, I think, that faded as the grapes brightened.

So much for the dark drawing-room.
So much for death-candles in the gloom.
At eighteen months of my life, grapes glowed
The green of greens, a light, a beatitude.

Mona

Mona turned all language to a comic
Amazement at catastrophe barely averted.
'My *gar*, Harold! What did you *do*?'
Round eyes puckering to chuckles at a new
Panic and wonder, 'My *life*,
HARold!' Left every phrase on the rise
Dazzled in its natural drama.

Nothing happened at the creek
That week each summer. I was puzzled
Why parents didn't need to play, just laugh
In tune with Mona's anguished shrieks
At Harry's bloodies and buggers as he guzzled
The fish he'd caught. The lamp lit,
Harry in bed, Mona did exercises,

Groaned, bumped and thumped, showed how far
Snapped suspenders sank back in the fat.
'I'n it *shameful!*' Whooped her anguish.
'Mona you're obscene.' Kneaded more flesh,
Found more. 'AMy!' chuckled and thumped. 'My *gar*!
Harold, did you *ever*!' I understood,
Half-asleep in my mother's lap,
Everything aquiver, it was good.

Harold

When you laughed, at your own joke or another's,
To the damned and God himself it carried.
Which came back to you, amplifying your laughter.
God shook then over all the wheatfields.
Making you throw your head back and split the ceiling.
God suffered agonies in his own chapels.
Back went your head, blasting the rooftops.
If it rained it was God's helpless tears.

Ben Wearne

'Think of his dear mother, she could 'ardly stan', crawlin'
About on 'er 'ands and knees, I expec' she was,
Beatin' 'er 'ead on the ground, 'cause 'er *dear Son*,
'Er dear *cheel*, was in hagony' (here his tears
Would well). 'How could hanybody *do* it to'n?

Look at'n there, upon the cross of glory,
His poor hands and feet, the dear of'm, the *dear* of'm...'
He made it sound not like an old story,
But like a real son – his own son.

Well, he is dead, I suppose, though I never heard,
And, I suppose, his native carn his cairn.
I hope they sent him off with his own tune, Blaenwaern.

Perry

Perry thought every country had a moon.
One moon per island. She was insular.
Over a brother's letter I saw her frown:
'Have they got the same moon in America?'

When Uncle John died, Perry shunned company,
Kept to the two-roomed house where she was born.
Stubbornly accomplished her suttee
Sitting for years at her cornish range, alone.

All sounds profaned her, church- or icecream bells.
Were it anything outside her, even grief,
It would have been a shocking waste of life.
But it was Perry's self, and nothing else.

Ready for a tart chat if anyone called,
Even pleased, I think; but readily inclined
To readmit the silence that appalled
Us with the weight of what we left behind:

Her hands folded, guarding the pearshaped growth
She would not have cut out; prodding the flame.
Stranger, holier, than art. So set to take
Possession of her death before it came.

The Match

He spent an hour on the old recreation ground
Kicking conversions from all angles,
Then, the light fading, explained to me the technique.

Did you know my father? I said.
Of course, he replied. I thought of him
Running, close to full-time, along the touch

Trilby-hatted trying to will the Reds
To score a try in the corner. *I haven't been
To a match for fifteen years*, I said. Old trench-

Face said, *Is it the violence, the kicking and
Gouging?* No I said *it's the death*, tears spurting
From my sleeping eyes, *it's the death, the death.*

Amy

Whispered to us, so he shouldn't overhear,
'It's Harold's cousin Bertie. He's deaf-and-dumb.'
Crying through laughter, laughing through tears,
Tears a reflection of happiness held within,
As Bertie held music, or as a creek
People liked coming to and birds sang around.

Stamps

Albums of laughing brethren on the *Berengaria*
Shoulder to shoulder slanting against the wind,
A bride or two among them, shielded like candleflames.

Family registers in great Bibles
Cherishing the still-born
As the pleiades their lost sister.

And the next of the same sex
Given the same name, living two lives.
The dead stamps still terribly thumps. Telegrams

From my Uncle Willie,
Stuck first in Tolima, then in Muswell Hill
With a nervous bloom: 'Holiday postponed. Belle ill.'

Auntie Cecie scuttling with the bad news
Flapping, from house to house. The sky dark
As the sunk granite terrace and beginning to drizzle.

The dead are simply in Santa Monica.
Remembering their birthdays,
The old aunts put stamps before food.

The Mixer

Freddie mixed cement, mixed metaphor
And reality. My father engaged by the boss
With recollections of the perils of typhus
In India – how you had to make sure,
When children went out with the nanny for the day,
All their water was boiled – Freddie took note,
Hunched over, and rose scornfully when he had gone.
'What a bleddy man, i'n it, 'Arold, what a bleddy man!
Sendin' his children out with a bleddy goat!'
Yet overhearing a nurse, stooped by a bed,
Say, 'You're very low,' Freddie came flying
Down the ladder, his cherubic round face grey:
'Bleddy nurse, just told a bleddy man he's dyin'.'

Is Freddie right, who was always wrong before?
Is Harold, dust-lagged, richer than Franz Hals'
Cavalier, throwing back his head
In laughter falling like cool dew on all
Who build whatever houses house the dead?

Stud

He's harvester among the carn rocks. Wives
Let him trump them after the village-drives.
What plums the moist flour when the widows bake?
Colours the shy maids, fruity as saffron cake?

Lighting up, he focuses the dry wit
Outside the chapel. Who looked ripe for it.
They rib him on the stains found in his car.
The evenings draw in. Winter's his threshing-floor.

A boyish chuckle in the grizzled stubble.
He had, when you were leaving home, or troubled,
A silence-covering way of saying 'Yes',
Several times over, with a gruff rising stress,

That consoled; and is loved like the brambled wheals,
Or the contours of snow clinging to some fields,
Farms, slopes, engine-houses and stacks,
Longer than others, when the east wind's backed

Atlantic-wards: each time the same shapes
Of determined white on the dark tilted landscape.
Autumn, he buys back what he's given: the chapel
Mellow with the firstfruits, wheat and apple,

The blessing crackling into auction, women
Ablaze with hats of violet, pink, lemon,
The preacher-auctioneer wrenching his stud
Off, in the spirit, his jolly face a blood-

Orange, Will offers wine-gums round the basses,
Grins wickedly down at the sea of faces,
Nods here and there, and bids first for the gross
Marrow, to shrieks in God's sweet granite house.

Sunday Evening

Eddie hovering, searching for one last loud
Chord, closing his eyes in bliss,
Hearing it fade in my father's soulful ending.
Leslie unveiling his score, a touch of class,
A refining fire, to his wife's ivory smile
Like a mild orgasm. Finger to lowered brow,
Retired Eddie's expressionless wink

At whoever caught his expression.
Cecie scuttling out to make the tea.
Nellie's 'Wonderful music', with a request
For 'Wanting You'. Eddie re-installed. Soaring
My mother as my father plunged. And plunged
As his carrot-haired cousin like a seraph soared
In 'Watchman what of the Night?':

Virginal middle-aged Owen, whose wild eyes
Conveyed the same amazement, whether he prayed
His beloved to come to his arms, in 'Nirvana',
'As the river flows to the ocean',
Or laughed at his own jokes without a sound.
Ethel deaf. None of them, thank God,
For Nirvana this time around.

The Honeymoon Voyage

We have felt lost before,
I tell your mother as the dead
Ship's engines nose through the silent
Mist, and her infirmity
Weakens as home slips further out of reach,
Carn Brea nor Basset Carn, two hills
Of ice slice past us, a monstrous floe

Drifting from Labrador.
The bunk that is our marriage-bed
Pitches through still more violence.
I kiss her tears, confetti
Thrown in a graveyard, her dark eyes beseech
Gentleness I give, our two wills
Melt again into one drifting flow,

And her eyes shine like ore
In the airless cabin. Her head
Lies on my shoulder. In her sigh, love
Leans back to you and pities
Your agony, but we lie each to each,
Wintered yet like your daffodils
Shooting early in the Cornish snow

Moist wind driving ashore
Is beginning to melt. Ahead,
I tell your mother's childlike
Vision, is Yosemite
Again, and the blue rollers of Long Beach,
The small home on Beverly Hills
I built for her, our first car you know

From photographs. Death's more
Beautiful, I tell her, than red-
woods, Sonora's wild lilac,
With a generosity
Warmer than Santa Clara's vale of peach-
trees and apricot, flanked by hills
The golden lemon verbenas grow

So lush on, Livermore...
Santa Monica and Merced,
San Francisco's Angel Island,
That creek, Los Alamitos,
Palm Springs...Didn't the sight of them outreach
My promise? Remember Soulsbyville's
Strange trees...our drive to Sacramento?

Trust me, I tell her, for
The last time I returned I led
You, little more than a child when
We parted, to a city
So wonderful it took away your speech...
And she trusts me, while her grief spills
Naturally with the honeymoon snow.

Voyage

Lych-gate upon her eyes, death cup her in hands
as tenderly as she would hold a sparrow,
pass here, the rich choices of a poor child,
pass here, the delicacy of a young girl,
sickness and health, her first sweet love bite:
who scolded me, who chose to ignore it,
a black-haired beauty then a white-haired beauty,
in her lap the whole ground, immovable,
my mother, here, my mother, here,
one solo dominates, I hear from habit,
one voice reiterates her tenaciously
like the lead stove she poked up, winter dawns.
Place she placed my father, waits to deflower
her, smooth away the knots of old age
and ways, fact of her death, pass here, way
to myself, gold ring to ring, voyagers
to America again, her seasick eases. Light,
four old men can bear, from boyhood knew them.

Flesh

Let me ache, indicate, simper who touched
your warm cunt, whisper, let on now,
disperse them into our love.
Who did you? it's all the same:
deep pricks or, islands of assiduous fictions,
disperse them into our love.

Am I in her, pummel her, he fucked you, ah
total and thousands of indecent, poked it in
did he, turgid and slewed, my girl, you right
there immixed with another, convoke it actually
wrapt round him, feel his engorgement
displacing your space, cleaving your achable
cleft better than this, novel then sweetly
a habit, why that's my spirit,
my fluttering clairvoyant, my fat ghost.

Sirmio

Pain, almost, an island's, almost-an-island's pain,
whether we turn in the same direction to sleep,
sleeping together drifting to together-
asleep, her arm loosely round me,
or whether nightly having loved and argued together
I take the onus of leaving, repugnant, peregrin,
a day older going down the same flights: where it's
blackest, the stars soon reform, a field of labourers,
salvagers, a million ovens baking in each one
gold as her window still on, unlidded eye, a lake, I
leaving, trees gusting, a torn nail could catch her room.

Venice

Like fiery glass we've twisted you
into our own fantastic shapes.
The corsets of your courtesans were nothing
to the bonds we've strapped you in. We've poured

you into paint and, the world's oldest ghetto,
made your windows face inwards on yourself.
I've heard your nightmares much too close for comfort,
and stretched a shaking hand for cigarettes.

Or can you, Venice, as I conceive this dissolute
and subtle lady, feed our dreams and create them
by being bound in your luridly chaste belt?
So that your lord himself, returning,

finds that your whole soul has reknit? Will you drown us?
Or shall we wake one day to find you are
the single tear on the cheek of the Torcello
virgin, that tall slim lady carrying God?

Portraits
(to the memory of Akhmatova)

Nothing visits the silence,
   No apparition of lilac,
      But an inexplicable lightness
         I sense when I breathe your name.
It's not All Souls'. The planet
   Spins on without you, Anna.
      You're now the Modigliani
         Abstract. No candles flame
To amass shadows. Light elected
   You. Annenkov's portrait...erect head
      That tilts with a swan's curve
Towards the Neva, towards the living
   Surge of the iced river

That will not stop nor swerve
But plunge, if need be, within you...
    Till room and time started spinning,
        I've gazed, I've tried to splinter
            With love that smiles at stone
This photo of nineteen-twenty,
    The only one where your tender
        Pure and gamine face, grown
One with the page you've entered,
    Blurs at the lips, half-surrenders
        A smile...And your lips open
            To me, or familiar Chopin...
                It must have been a dream.
But dreams are something substantial,
    The Blue Bird, the soft embalmer.
        It doesn't smell of catacombs
There, and your black fringe is no nimbus.
    A cathedral bell tolls dimly.
        The unmoving stylus hums.
So deep has been this trance,
    Surely its trace fell once,
        Caught your eyes and startled you,
Between the legendary embankment
    And your House on the Fontanka?

        I, like the woman who
Had touched the healer's soul,
    Find everything made whole
        In your poetry's white night,
Envy the poor you kept watch
    With, outside the prison; the touch
        Of a carriage-driver, your slight
Hands bearing down with a spring, one
    Moment in the tense of his fingers.
        Poems outlive a Ming vase,
            But your ageing portraits bring me
            The rights of a relative
To grieve. Tonight alone I could spare
    All that is written here
        To restore the chaos where
            The Neva deranges your hair,
                You laugh, weep, burn notes, live.

Orpheus in Hell
(in memory O.M.)

Perhaps if he praised Death?...
They might spare her.
But what came to him was a flight of starlings.

He had never known such torture.
He dragged in a writing-desk,
He sharpened a pencil, laid out a sheet

Of white paper, and made himself sit.
But before he could find a line about Death
He was up and pacing the close and lightless

Room and his lips were moving
Joyfully, his image of her
As the earth's menstruation

Had started up an image of poppy-fields
Blowing red in the clean wind.
He ground his teeth

And made himself sit down again
At the hideous blank paper
And she tried to help him concentrate

By pretending to be asleep
Since it was impossible for her to walk out
And leave his lips free to compose.

He tried to praise her death,
But he was up and pacing on his worn shoes
With a lyric of how her warm lips couldn't

Hide their wakefulness, and she opened her eyes
And smiled, and, smiling, he groaned,
Sat down at the desk and scrawled something.

And in time his Ode to Death saved her.
They were content to keep him only.
She rose to life with a whole notebook of poems

That had seeped like immortal living gum
Out of the dead wood of his death ode,
And every morning she ran it through

In her memory, and every night,
So that the trees and rocks still moved with it.

The Marriage of John Keats and Emily Dickinson
in Paradise

This is no dream, the soul is flying south.
Further in summer than the grass,
And past the fields of gazing grain,
And past the stubble-fields of Ruth,
The cold hill side opens, your breast's a flame.

Shiver, a loaded gun.
The throat's a nightingale too full to sing.
Eternal lids apart,
Your eyes the colour of the sherry
Left by the parting guest.

I died for beauty, you for truth.
Fret not after knowledge, I have none.
Experiment escorts us last.
One Gabriel and one Sun
Protect our armouries;
For love is all there is.

The Substance

What is this substance I call glass
she makes? Invisibility
only one side of which I touch.
When I breathe on it I see,
between myself and all I am,
her name, transparently.

Where we slept the facing wall
is a redoubling of the glass
she makes – invisible
but with a ghost's reflectiveness,
the inside of a crystal ball,
the past and all it meant to us

and means: a painful incompletion
I discover was complete.
Once, the substance came by chance
apart in my hands and gave a fleet
and overwhelmingly recalling
fragrance of her I'll not repeat.

A crack ignorable and sheer
in something I can't get behind
that a wind shakes from roof to floor
catches the noon and makes me blind.
Books allow my hand so near,
needle and thread I cannot find.

The Young King Prophesies Immortality
(St Ethelbert)

Never shall the bride-sleep fall on me.
This index nail's white bruise, and my arm
Numb from sprawling reading Origen.

'Know that you are another world in miniature,
And in you are the sun, the moon, and also the stars...'
Know too that death is a matter of depth
Within the apartment-house of limitless storeys
That stretches around the curved shore
Of a desolate lake. Do you fear eviction? Yet
Were you ever *not* here? You look out over the dark lake
From your own window, shivering at the silence.
But to the flier whose shadow skims the lake,
St Michael or Garuda, all the lights,
On all the floors, are blazing...

Elegy for Isabelle le Despenser

*At Tewkesbury Abbey is a lock of red-brown hair, belonging
to Isabelle, Countess of Warwick, and dated 1429*

Better than stones and castles were my bones.
Better than spears and battles were my tears.
Better than towers and rafters was my laughter.
Better than light and stained glass was my sight.
Better than grate and boar-spit was my hate.
Better than rush and tapestry was my flush.
Better than gold and silver was my shiver.
Better than gloves and falcons was my love.
Better than hymns and pilgrims were my limbs.
Better than crests and banners were my breasts.
Better than tombs and effigies was my womb.
Better than art and ikons was my hurt.
Better than crypts and candles were my friendships.
Better than leaf and parchment was my grief.
Better than mass and matins was my chatter.
Better than swans and bridges were my yawns.
Better than wool and weaving was my breathing.

Remember Isabelle le Despenser,
Who was as light and vivid as this hair.
We are all one.
She sees the clouds scud by, she breathes your air,
Pities the past and those who settled there.

Vienna. Zürich. Constance.

*In May 1912 Freud visited the town of Constance, near Zürich, to
spend a weekend with a sick colleague. Jung was deeply hurt that he
had not taken the opportunity to visit him in Zürich; Freud equally
so that the younger man had not come to see him in Constance.
Their relationship, already strained, ended abruptly soon after.*

It was a profound unmeeting.
The train on the branchline from Zürich to Constance
Held a carriage which held a compartment
With a white seat-cover with an impression of Dr Jung,
Slit eyes, in a pugnacious bullet head,
By no means the merry young man of his old age.

The young woman opposite, bright
In a black-and-white striped dress, a blue neck-scarf,
Did not chat to the man not clutching his briefcase
But read through the short journey, smiling occasionally,
Nor did she follow him out at Constance
Where he was warmly embraced by an older man.

The train on the branchline from Constance to Zürich
Held a carriage which held a compartment
With a white seat-cover with an impression of Dr Freud,
His face graven with battles, genial-eyed.
The young man opposite in a modern, very
Tight brown suit with a heavy Victorian watch-chain

Was not startled by the old gent not leaning forward
And not telling him with a twinkle why he had stammered
Momentarily over the word Constance,
But rubbed his hands dreamily and gazed out.
Nor did he help him with his case at Zürich
Where he was greeted cordially by his son.

By a strange coincidence
The young woman who would have been in Jung's compartment
Had Jung been travelling, was the mistress
Of the young man who would have been in Freud's compartment
Had Freud been travelling. Having confused
Their plans, they passed each other, unaware.

Waiting for him in her hotel at Constance,
The young woman stepped out of her rainy clothes.
Her fur hat momentarily became a vulva.
Waiting for her in his hotel at Zürich,
The young man stared irritably out of the window
And saw an uncanny light pass across the sky.

Emma and the children leaving the table,
The sage head darkly reflected in its polish
Did not gracefully accept the modified libido theory.
Gazing into the waters of Lake Constance,
A fatherly hand resting on his shoulder,
Jung did not smilingly abjure his mystical drift.

Freud dined sombrely with the faithful Binswanger,
And pleaded a headache. Jung worked late. Owls hooted.
In their uneasy sleep the two exchanged their dreams.
Snow fell on the Jungfrau. Lenin dreamlessly slept.
The centuries slowly drifted away from each other.
In Emma's kitchen-drawer a knifeblade quietly snapped.

In Her Imagined Person

Why – all senses roused – is he deaf, is he blind?
– Not that deepest darkness is all black,
Even in Shakespeare's black play, his twenty-fourth;
Nor that the exquisite rack
Never drags out the truth
In which she lies, madonna playing whore,

Through her betraying, all too faithful voice;
Though limbs may work like thieves
With time against them
To dynamite a door;
Though desire is a magician's sleeves
Where what he wills, he finds,–

For eyes adjust to midnight,
Even without stars and moonlight,
Even without window-frames,
Enough to tell the particular star
That has fallen, leaving its ice-world, and melted
Into your arms.

It's just that there's no arguing with
The stubborn girl, eternity.
Shy as snowfall, trembling
Like a full cup not to be dashed aside,
And with more rents than a tree,
She will come rustling, keen-eyed, to her choice

Unworthy of this rape, and naked slide
Her breath to his so close it is his own,
And he surrenders all to her surrender,
The unrecognised, the known,
Heartless, and tender,
The stranger and the bride.

Stone

The first book of a poet should be called *Stone*
Or *Evening*, expressing in a single word
The modesty of being part of the earth,
The goodness of evening and stone, beyond the poet.

The second book should have a name blushing
With a great generality, such as *My Sister Life*,
Shocking in its pride, even more in its modesty:
Exasperated, warm, teasing, observant, tender.

Later books should withdraw into a mysterious
Privacy such as we all make for ourselves:
The White Stag or *Plantain*. Or include the name
Of the place at which his book falls open.

There is also the seventh book, perhaps, the seventh,
And called *The Seventh Book* because it is not published,
The one that a child thinks he could have written,
Made of the firmest stone and clearest leaves,

That a people keep alive by, keep alive.

Lorca

Lorca
walking
in a red-light
district at night
heard one of his own songs
being sung
by a whore

he was moved
as if the stars
and the lanterns
changed places

neither the song
to himself
belonged
nor the girl
to her humiliation
nothing
belonged to anyone

when she stopped singing
it went on

death must be a poor thing
a poor thing

DREAMING IN BRONZE
(1981)

The Stone Clasp

Donna Anna, I don't know how to say this.　·
Briefly and shamefully, I cannot come.
I should, at this moment, be face to face with you
in your own house; a privilege you've granted
to no one since your husband died, and which
I've striven with all my soul to draw from you,
deliriously obsessed with you; last night
our brief tryst at your house inflamed me more.
Yet now, I can't come. No, not can't, but won't.
The events of the past days are like a dream.
Banished for my crime, I stole back, as
you know, and watched you nightly visit your
late husband, the Commander's, grave. I wooed you
stealthily in the guise of a monk, and won you
– good and virtuous lady – to grant me that hour
of converse in your sad house. There I declared
my true identity: your husband's slayer,
vile, dissolute Don Juan; said I loved you,
and that this unknown word, love, might redeem me.
I bared my heart to your knife. Tormented by
the claims of honour and your still fresh love
for the Commander, you forgave me; I
begged for one cold and quiet kiss: you gave it,
and by your silence granted my entreaty
that I return this evening. Donna Anna,
I picture you in your room of crucifixes,
eyeing the clock, trembling, wondering if I've
been caught and murdered by your husband's friends.
But I am here with Laura, warm and safe.
Probably because of your seclusion
you won't have heard of her. She's a fine actress,
and my true friend. She's trying to read this
over my shoulder. She's but a child – eighteen –
yet older than you, my angel, in experience;
during my exile she's lain here with hundreds
(she protests I exaggerate grossly: well,
with several). Her breasts are exquisite.

I'll tell you how it is. When you allowed
my lips to brush yours in that marble kiss,

the rest became inevitable. By
midnight tonight, I'd be a traveller
in that familiar, unknown country you
cherish, hardly aware of, in your lap,
beneath your black dress of perpetual mourning.
In spite of, or because of, your pure soul,
it would have been inevitable, and
I think you know it. It would be easy to
pretend I'm saving you by my not coming;
but that is not my motive. Nor would it
be right to say I anticipate the bored
satiety of conquest. No, I'd want
to plunge again and again into your being,
Donna Anna. I can see no end to love.
Dearest creature, when I said I loved you,
I thought I lied. But when I left last night,
I saw the stone Commander, in your porch,
your husband's marble statue, and I knew
I loved you indeed. He planted his heavy hand
in mine, and nodded gravely. I recalled
your eyes, sombre with sorrow and with passion,
and in them I saw death for the first time.
I have killed many, but never till last night
did I see death. It was in your eyes,
and in the stone Commander's clasp. My love,
Donna Anna, lying side by side
night after night, with every heartbeat we
would dig our grave, erect our marble tomb.
I'd rather Laura's gay and carnal paintings,
her multitude of blazing torches, each
like one of her lovers; her unstinted wine;
the occasional sparkling song to the guitar;
the way, when we have finished fucking (you
should know this crudity: it's Juan), she
tosses her hair, and laughs, and tells me about
the lovers she's had, and I tell her about mine.
Tomorrow I shall leave Madrid again,
and if I ever return – only for Laura.
I shall remember you with reverent love;
but don't remember me – or not with love;
keep all your prayers and tears for the Commander.
I don't want your stone clasp about my heart.

Farewell, My Life; I Love You

1

Your letter has touched me with its simple meaningless phrases,
its strokes as clear as stars in this summer sky,
as pointless and serene, my love, my fate.
Beneath the absolute beauty of your surfaces
there is nothing, nothing, Natalia. That is why
I love you. To love you is to learn to skate.

The deepest thing about you is your pearls,
those creatures of the sea who rest between
the marble, soft, exquisite, lifeless mountains
– my hermitages, after the soulful girls
whose kisses were quicker than lizards in green
gardens of fig trees and eternal fountains.

I love the emptiness of your smile, your slow
wit, your foolish chatter. A child, I play
in your suburban street, before carriages
and crowds have smutched it, after the first snow;
you dazzle me, and that is how you'll stay
after many childbearings and miscarriages.

I shall come to you without fail, in autumn, soon.
Do you understand? I shall come at the year's fall.
My name is the only word I need to hear –
without turning to me your face, the vapid moon.
It is miracle enough that you speak at all
or comb at all your magnificent black hair.

I hunger for you to touch me absently;
your tolerant indifference does not hurt
any more. I will hover above you
hoping for a sign of life in your perfectly
still face, but happy to feel your beating heart.
Farewell, my life; I love you.

2

Dizzily the pines fly past;
sorrowful, the confused soul
is half determined to turn back
along the already buried track,
but fearfully, out of control
she is borne on by the sleigh's
joyful momentum and the hollow
ache in her throat she cannot swallow
It's silent. Round the only rays,
maddened, helpless in the circle
of its unrest, the blizzard swarms;
her eyes are hot as candleflames;
the sky is heavy with the weight
of whiteness deepening the night;
she thinks the way ahead is home,
the girl is in delirium;
now she is losing consciousness;
but the sleigh sings on cracking ice,
knowing the water to be crossed,
knowing her longing to be lost
in love tonight and sacrificed.

The title occurs in one of Pushkin's letters to his wife Natalia.

Fathers, Sons and Lovers
(Vienna, 1919)

TAUSK – FREUD *(letter)*

Dear Freud. I have arranged to go at one
daily to Frau Deutsch. She is yours at three,
I gather, and at noon she feeds her son.
Your letter came as a surprise to me,
I must confess. I fear I had presumed,
in view of my long service to the cause
and, above all, to you, you'd have assumed
the burden of my analysis. I was
a little shaken, wondering what offence
I'd given. But since you've taken her
yourself, a rare mark of her excellence
in your regard, I'm calmer, happier
about unmasking my mind's violence.

FREUD – HELENE DEUTSCH *(analysis)*

She thanks you for the goat's milk. Bring your son,
now he is weaned, to visit her some time –
my wife would like that; stop her brooding on
my careless ash!...A candle in a lime
tree: beautiful, so rich! I catch a gleam
of light, at last, at last. I think we ought
to keep on, after all. And yet you seem
held back still, somehow. When you came, I caught
a scent – yes, yes, I know – but more like musk.
Don't let him drain you of all energy.
How near the end are you? Take care. His tusk
has ploughed through women before, to get to me.
They're not the fruit he craves, simply the husk.

I bring you greetings from my mother-in-law;
you were a fellow-student, I believe.
Your Paper, last night, on dementia
was brilliant; I regret I had to leave
before the end – my child was ill. I write
to plead with you to use your influence
with Freud. I know my stumbling thoughts are trite,
but he can't keep awake. I have a sense
of sickness, self-destructive gloom. Please make
him rest a little, take a holiday.
He seems afraid of Tausk. I cannot break
that man's resistance. Compelling, though, the way
his eyes flash up and hold one, like a snake!

LOU SALOMÉ – FREUD

In Russia, with my husband and my lover,
I sensed, beneath our private turbulence,
a violence the deep ice could not cover,
and I am not surprised by these events.
Rilke was plunged in gloom. I gave him there
the symbol that he later used so well –
a panther circling endlessly its despair.
I sense it now in Tausk – an animal.
You know the unimaginable splendour
men can invest a hair, a shoe, a glove;
yet Tausk – so good a soul – will not surrender,
even to himself, the covenant of his love,
and so is cruellest where he feels most tender.

113

FREUD – LOU SALOMÉ

How the still night conceals Vienna's hurts!
I love the lights reflecting on the water,
our quiet strolls, the rustle of your skirts.
Yes, talk to Anna, if you would; my daughter
should be less tied to me. My friend, our talks
heal me at day's end. I'm hacking through
a lonely, perilous jungle. Nietzsche stalks
there too, ahead. And Rilke – yes. Frau Lou,
I'd like to rest, but too much is at stake.
I feel my age. The death-wish theory rose
out of a dream I had. A small grass snake
punctures my brow and, as I weaken, grows.
A python haunts the path it knows I'll take.

LOU SALOMÉ – TAUSK *(letter)*

My friend, what can I say? Poor Victor! Brother-
animal! The life of a great man is fraught,
demonic. Freud could not endure another
creative mind frustrating his own thought.
Unquestioningly she would obey him – so
besotted is she. Think: poor *Sigmund!* Is
it not, after all, more moving than chilling to know
he has reached greatness through his frailties?
Think of your bride-to-be; you're not alone.
And though I slept with you because you were
close to the master, as you must have known,
you'll find no friend who's truer, tenderer.
That was our house of straw, but this is stone.

TAUSK – FREUD *(letter)*

Kindly give aid to Fräulein Loewi, one
created to be a pure and loving wife.
I would have failed her, as I failed, as son
and father, lover and husband, all my life.
I must do this thing right, and to that end
will noose the curtain-cord around my throat
and put the pistol to my brow. My friend,
dying is good, it is an antidote
to all our ills, it is great joy to climb
out of my animal skin. The linden trees
are singing. For everything, I thank you; I'm
honoured that I knew you. Yours. Tausk. Please,
also look after my sons from time to time.

*Victor Tausk, 1879-1919, was one of Freud's most talented
and experienced followers. After a decision that all analysts
must themselves be analysed, Freud appointed Helene
Deutsch, a young newcomer, as Tausk's analyst; while he
himself analysed Frau Deutsch. At Freud's prompting, she
broke off Tausk's analysis mid-way. Deprived of his last frail
link with the master, Tausk committed suicide. The fourth
person in the poem, Lou Andreas-Salomé, was the gifted
friend or mistress of Nietzsche, Rilke, Freud and Tausk.*

Peter Kürten to the Witnesses
(Düsseldorf, 1931)

I have too much a sense of being alive
to take the guillotine in another way
than as the cause of an erection.
I've lived, dreading reprieve, anticipating
the ecstasy of hearing my own blood gush.
It's true, and I don't want pity.

One night I roamed the Hofgarten lake,
in a desperate condition, but found only a swan,
and cut its head off while it slept.
It's chilly. I won't be long. If I were you
I'd be anticipating the orgasm, like the day
I saw a mangled horse.

I can smell blood a mile off and I'm certain
the hour is at hand when you will say,
why did we kill good Peter Kürten?
But it's as well. I should be much too soft;
for the time came when I grew tired,
felt I could do no more.

I'm sorry about the children, and especially
little Gertrude, she took my hand so trustingly.
I loved children and they loved me.
As the Prosecutor said, I am – I am –
I am rather a nice man. And a shy man.
My stammer gets worse when I'm keyed up. I'm sorry.

I desperately wanted all the women who came
with me, so willingly, not to be upset
but to share the pleasure, to share
the absurd comedy of my dropping behind
on the path, lassooing them suddenly, dragging
them over the earth.

Everyone's been most kind. I've put on weight.
If I were free, I'd kill you all. All Düsseldorf
still wouldn't be enough.
And yet, you know, there were times I dreamed
I'd capture the Monster, and be fêted
by my grateful fellow-citizens!

You're welcome to my brain, gentlemen
of the University; I'll think of you
slicing it like tripe, saying
there's Maria Hahn, and there's Rose Ohliger,
etcetera, etcetera, and here is our answer.
But that would surprise me.

I could tell you it was my father raping
my mother and my sister, ten of us in one room,
or being taught to torture
and masturbate dogs, but it's deeper than that,
it's what I am, through eternity, therefore
I must thank God who doesn't exist.

Be good to my wife. She never knew the mayhem in
our bed. That was heroic of me. I wrote
last night to all the next-of-kin.
I'm grateful also for the many fine love-letters
women have sent to me – perhaps your own wives.
Thank you for seeing me off.

The Wolf-Man

Five white, snowy-white wolves
sat silent on Christmas tree branches
in the dream given me on my fourth
birthday, on the eve of Christmas.

They sat erect, their ears pricked,
as innocent as cats. One
I had seen through the bars of my cot,
the wolf called Love, my parents

in their siesta, the white underclothes,
the furred mouth, the striking tongue.
Or did I see dogs coupling? Many times
he has come, in the form of servants

scrubbing floors. And the others came.
The wolf called Death, many times
that whelp of Love has howled
without sound outside my window.

And his half-brother, the wolf Suicide.
Twice I have seen him; now in my sister's
nightgown, now in my wife's.
He is the cunning and malicious one.

The wolf Madness I have seen,
the one with the pocket-mirror.
And the wolf Terror,
who stalked Odessa and Vienna,

at first a quiet shadow, then openly
snatching babies from prams.
Happy the man of eighty
who has seen only five wolves.

The 'Wolf-Man' was one of Freud's most famous patients.

Anastasia Questioned

I don't know who I am. Perhaps I am
the ikon lamp they lit for me at birth,
the pure gold, melted down to feed
all the poor people on the poor earth.
I have been bled white as Alexei's skin,
as the white sky behind these winter trees
meshed beyond identity. I'm in
a nightmare where I wake to a bad room,
making the sign of the cross, embracing each other,
waiting for death to come, the bolshevik.
I am all the poor people on the poor earth.
I am not what I say, and yet the sea
cannot contain the tears
that have blotted out my memory.
I am the charred clothes and the severed finger,
corset-bones underground and the pet dog.
I'm the dumb girl dragged out of a canal,
and I am running towards trees,
raped by my captors, struck violent blows.
I'm in a closed train heading for Kazan
with Mama and my sisters. Mama! Marie!
Where are you? I am wherever you are.
I'm in the family group of peasants by
the woodpile Papa has just chopped up.
We're smiling, huddled, and the picture snows.
The century's stretched me out, a flight of cranes,
no landmark in the featureless snow reminds
me of my name.

Life has touched me like Rasputin's kiss
and I'm too simple-minded to be sure
I don't survive. I think I am the wind
playing around the entrance to the shaft
over which four pine trees used to thresh
called the Four Brothers. I am the spirit-lamp
I dressed by at Ipatiev, shivering,
the clock that went on ticking, burnt to ash.

Revisiting Arizona

1

For a year I planned to revisit Arizona,
to purify my spirit again
in the desert's holy stillness;
to renew my acquaintance with the tarantula
in the Desert Museum,
and my love-affair with a girl whose hair
was like a downpour of the desert sun.

I supposed it would be a different tarantula.
I don't know how long a tarantula lives.
I would press my nose again against its glass,
and outstare it: those vastly subhuman eyes,
that steel inertia, squat
in the midst of its repulsive, bristling legs,
poised to leap in the service of its hunger
to remain forever a tarantula.

The girl, too, would not be the same,
nor the unchanging desert of buttes and cactus,
because I am seven years older.
But I would renew my soul
in the boiling dust-bowl, between mountains,
where the tarantulas roam free.

At the last minute I cancelled my flight,
having a premonition of disaster, a flying-fear.
Yet I have been flying there so long in my mind
that I've been hurled forward, as a crashed
pilot is impacted into his panel.
I have not seen the girl,
but I have seen the tarantula,
I have stared into its eyes,
an inch away, behind glass,
in its steamy prison, its brooding soul.

2

And since it is impossible to imagine flesh,
the flesh I would enter, warm and palpitating,
I have imagined your breasts as the snowcapped mountains of Sonora,
your hair as solar energy,
the desert our bed
shimmering and steamy with awesome life, yet cooling
into a night tree of serene brilliant stars,
and your vagina as the dark shafts
of Arizona and Mexico where my Cornish fathers
sought copper and silver.

For weeks I have imagined them, trembling
towards the moment when myth
would be ripped away like a polaroid's skin.
The stretchedapart bucking thighs, the acrid
and desirable tang, the wet strand
I'd peel from my mouth. But you are still
the limitless Sonora, and our meeting
is a question for the rattlesnake in his coiled dream.

My Sister's War

From flight-decks of the Cornish moor
the braves each night hit our dull town
where, gallant boys, they fell in flames,
dazzled by an auburn sun.
A quickfire Hurricane and dressed
to kill, safe between granite breasts,
my sister had a marvellous war.

The blitz on Plymouth was no more
than a charmed backcloth to romance,
faint slender searchlights gliding round,
too far away to cause alarm,
grave nightly rituals without sound,
an orange glimmer, while she necked
with the elect of the elect.

They were in transit, and they went.
One shy Flight Sergeant lasted ten
fog-grounded days, and wrote thereafter
religiously. We saw her when
she flew in and flew out. Seventeen,
she was, God knows, as innocent
as the wise virgins of the screen:

keeping her legs, she chuckled, crossed.
Then the Yanks came. Beware, beware,
our parents said, the older man.
The Major's face was like our coast.
Oh, but they set the town alight,
danced *In the Mood*, night after night
until the second front began;

and planned to have two children later.
She wrote her Anzac navigator
Dear John...but never sent it; for
just then his photo came, how deeply
true were his eyes, our parents said;
and Lois, spinning, banking steeply,
ditched her Texan guy instead.

Peace brought her Anzac fiancé,
and it was fine. Still starry-eyed,
she packed her trunk. The people whom
she loved stood clustered in the room;
the taxi came. We waved. She cried.
And only then a night-attack
surprised her heart, and all went black.

Big Deaths, Little Deaths

1

Late April, '34. Don Bradman drove
to 96, leaving the weary cover
standing, then the day's play was over.
Slept like an angel. Didn't see clouds move
across the stars, eastwards. Westward, love
was blindly choosing out of sperm and ova
two that knit and held. A low cloud-cover
made the ball swing both ways, but the Don clove
cover and mid-off, having read the flight,
and lifted his cap. Something I know as I
was suddenly here that morning – broke
into the universe, I don't know why,
why it was I, on that particular night,
rain starting to fall, her dark field, his dark stroke.

2

Drew a neat hole. Perhaps my uncle, who
had sailed from Cornwall, west, to mine for tin
before he joined the church, was thinking of
the holes he'd drilled to plug explosives in.
Resting on my cricket book, he sketched
an arc. I must have shown my awe. Could jet,
he smiled, half-way across the room.
He flew home to the States. Then the deep snows
of '47; packing, leaving our house,
bound for Australia. Over the round sea
we went. I wept. There were mysterious

lights on the water, white incandescent stars
as I wept for our ginger cat, a man pulled
at the loose tie of a blushing girl's white robe
in the ship's library, I felt a stir, a
fattening ache like tears, a spill of globes.

3

My sister's hubby shooed me from the lounge,
he didn't like the way I watched her thighs
kick off the fat. I didn't like the dark,
it soaked in ghosts and spiders like a sponge,
so took to creeping to my parents' room,
and mother turned out. I slept in father's sweat.

One night the stocky Anzac, a shock ape,
opened their door as I stole past, reeled back.
I was looking for the *Sporting World*, I said.
He loped away to the shower, muttering,
swinging his meat. One day I glimpsed her snatch.
It haunted me for weeks, a mote, a bat.
Asked if I knew about sex, but should have said
Brother I'll show you what it's all about
(I nearly asked her to, it seemed okay)
spreadeagled while the swinging ape was out.

4

Moon became sun, I came up wet from dreams,
tarantula on the wall, beast on my skin
more terrifying, fat, an atom-bomb.
So much white magic and no stage-assistant,
how could I use this power, if I was in
the flat alone, but breathe her murky scents,
and coil her belt around me, shivering.
A silken, tidal pull like homesickness.
My first affair, intense, unconsummated, –
a girl's cool, whispering thighs, a unicorn trapped
in the virgin's lap. Jesus, I choked
in flames I had no way of putting out,
that scorched and tickled in my aching throat.

My padded crop-haired tart, you taught me how
love meshes tighter as it strains apart,
the art of breathing when you're cut in two.

5

Too late – our sailing-date. Too early – I was fat,
tongue-tied. I cut her picture from the *Age*:
Snow-loving Sara Sukiert at Mount Thredbo.
Everything arrowed to her slender nape,
boyish black hair. When she returned the borrowed
notes, I stroked the page, an intercourse
beyond joy. Come to my woman's breasts...
but when she read the words the room was still.

The space you walked in wondered where you were.
We shook hands gravely and for weeks I cried.
Where did the milk go, Sara? Can't think of you
a plump grey kosher mama, or stretching wide
your legs that danced on flowers past my desk.
Ringing friends once, I said All the best
for Christmas, then remembered they were Jews.
Perhaps he's sucked at Sara's loving breast.

6

Marlene Dietrich taught me to masturbate,
the blue angel Nazi with her black belt
threw me, as I stood up, threw a switch
enough to jet a rainbow through the screen.
I hobbled to the Cambridge summer evening
and couldn't wait to try it for myself.
Nearly twenty. I developed late.

More deaths than in the purge of Leningrad,
and the siege, under the army blanket,
I learnt the Russian words for tank and shell.
A big girl from an eye infirmary
said tentatively we could try withdrawal,
harpooned on the sofa by my fingers,
but I was scared, I guess, also engaged.
Also she couldn't cure my squint.
Dragging them closer strained my eyes apart.

7

I rested my forehead against dark glass.
In a lighted window of a facing wing
I saw a nurse brush slowly her long hair.
She must have been thinking of the long
routine ahead, or planning what to wear
for a date. I went back in. The male-nurse
at his wrist guessed it would be ten minutes.

That was twenty years ago. But I do not forget her.
In fact, every day I see her, the slow
stroke of the brush down through her hair, facing
the dark dawn like a mirror; standing there
at the world's end, but wholly unaware,
wholly in the heartless serene world.

8

Such cheerful get-well cards came in, that morning,
I kept thinking he might still pull through.
Buses still ran, lights still worked. She refused
a sleeping-pill, saying she might not wake.
She said to close our eyes, though it was dark,
I heard the metals of her corset shake,
for we three huddled in one bed that night
as the right thing, giggling till we slept.
All the dead sleep the knife bit in my gut.

Mother had crept downstairs. I heard her prod
the chirks to ash, an iron dawn glimmered,
I drummed sperm and stayed hard, inside
my wife, a bankrupt drawing love, chuckling,
poking. I'd bring him back alive, by God I would.

9

I couldn't take another funeral
so soon, my baby-sitter took her school-
skirt off, no more: but this was generous.
I could do anything in her virginal
grid of flesh and fabric except fuck.

The sun edged to the sheet and faded back.
Silence was quieter than it should have been.
Her death had stretched, and made a hairline crack
in everything under the sun, and even the sun.
I thought of her surprised there was no work,
she for whom the chores were never done,
and never had a man. Now suddenly
she rasped her briefs down at the last. I'd thrust
against the black deniers, till I was raw,
too sore and angry now, the flower she grasped
and tried to help me force into the gash.

10

Unsuckable tits, her teeth dropping grips,
skirls of laughter as she combed and set
her tutor's wife's hair, I stooped to run
my hand up her skirt when that tremor went
across the screen that's still not stopped –
Kennedy shot. Expert with tongue and lips,
she tuned me to a pitch of keening want
beyond the range of dogs, the frequency
of outer space, her sleek, fugitive cunt.

A touch of her cool fingers was enough.
I laughed hysterically. And she – then cried.
Let me sleep with her only when she slept.
Her parents away. Needed to bring me home
to the terraces of rain, the pall of smoke,
sad chapels. I understood. It was love
unwove her in the night, her lashes wet.

11

They are double-agents exchanged at a border
it's snowing from a grey sky on to black fields
they climb out of black cars

they are terribly tired
of wondering whom they betray
even God does not know whom they betray
they avoid looking into their own eyes

because they have been lovers, or are lovers,
and know only that their hearts are cassette-recorders
and their eyes microfilms, at his hip a pistol
in her black nylon a white ice-pick

yet they won't assassinate – high on cyanide,
implacable tongues nursing the breakable capsules.

Ghost-House

I have made a ghost-house of black thread,
black wire. It swings like a birdcage,
a home to house the restless, perturbed dead.
And indeed they have found rest. We both believe
whatever haunts this bedroom with its breath
is breathing quietly and has ceased to grieve.

We think there are two. No, there are squares of two,
infinities of death.
Now while we sleep, the children cannot sleep,
they have to have one too. From their lamp-shade,
black thread and wire, it hangs, as beautiful
and intricate as the one my hands have made.

Suitcases

There are millions of suitcases in the world,
but my mother, at the end, didn't have one.
The nurses at her nursing home
found she had almost too many possessions
to pack into her three string bags,
but they succeeded.
No! there was also a carrier-bag
waiting for me with the others.
The makers of suitcases
never cut any ice with my mother.

Smile

The smile is already there
in the first snap, let's say seventeen,
under the mop of black
fuzzy ringlets, sitting an the back
steps of a granite cottage
in a Cornish village

the smile is still there
decorative as a film-star
at the wheel of a model-T
(my father in drainpipe trousers
proudly draped against them both)
in front of a spanish-white
bungalow in California

and is there, in the same white
place and in the same sunny
era, my sister in her arms,
and is there
under her early-grey hair
sitting on a donkey
on a Cornish beach

and is there
on a bright January day
having tea outside
with her sisters-in-law
and my grandmother
while I stare solemnly
at my first-birthday candle

and the smile is there
under tight white curls
in a Melbourne park,
a plump floral woman
by my plump floral sister
and I a fat youth poking his tongue

and is there, in the last snap
of my father, colour kodak,
on a Cornish quay, and is there
behind her glasses, hiding pain,
under thinning white hair
on her last holiday with us

and now that she is dead and gone,
having smiled in the undertaker's hut
so I shouldn't feel guilty,
and now that her death has faded
like the snaps,
the smile is still there,
some poems have no beginning and no end.

Two Women, Made by the Selfsame Hand

Each day I'd come back to the statuette,
the boy-girl, sturdy, nude, her elfin head
turned to the right, rejecting, yet
teasingly tilted; sensual and sad;
I'd touch my wallet, let it go; her hand
offered with upturned palm what it concealed.
She'd laugh at my uncertainty, and stand
admiringly before a Mother and Child:

– my friend, I mean; my more than friend. Our days
of rainy holiday were haunted by
a girl with briny locks and changeling gaze,
the left hand open on her thigh,
late-adolescent undine perching on
a rock – and her soulful primitive
madonna, tall and standing, gazing down
with all the fear that perfect love can give.

One hand sustained, the other curved around
the shell that held the whole of life, too brittle.
Oh but she wanted it! and would have found
the money for it, if *he* were not so little,
if his curious little hands weren't everywhere...
I watched her fade back through her gaze to hug
the absent child who is always there.
He'd break it, wouldn't he?...I shrugged

away her unbearable, unexpressed
question, and saw how disappointingly
the nude had changed again; the small pert breasts
and rounded thighs still pulled, but yesterday
her face was not so coarse nor so
malign, the fingers playing with a strand
more natural. I left the studio
for the last time, downcast; but looked back and

the girl was following; she wanted me
to have her, she said; her upturned palm
gestured with such a brazen subtlety,
her delicate grieving features held such charm,
I paused by the harbour, strode back, and got her.
She laughed at my confusion, glanced farewell
obliquely at the other terracotta,
followed me, and we drove to our hotel,

where doubts are cast aside: she draws my soul
into her numinous clay; our mingled smoke
broods on the irresponsible
tilted head under lamplight as we joke
about that open, all-accepting hand
hiding her sex. I say it means, *how much?*...
It means, she says, *get stuffed*...We undress and
lie down as straight as effigies. I touch

at length her hand, her closed thighs, the uncouth
wires I prise apart, as mad for her
as in her playful and affectionate youth.
She tilts away her head, and does not stir.
I turn her mouth to mine, but it stays lax.
I hear the sisters talking in her blood,
the nurturing madonna without sex,
the lonely mistress without motherhood.

They greet across my flesh, across the bay
between the studio and our hotel bed.
Almost before I've pulled away
she's lit a cigarette, her sculpted head
talks to itself in a calm monotone;
the hands, she says, of neither piece are right;
the hands...the hands are wrong...I lie like stone,
hearing her cut deep fractures from the night.

Poetry and Striptease

Poetry and Striptease, said the London Entertainments Guide;
but when I flipped to that heart-stunning page,
the Soho strip-clubs weren't offering poetry,
and the Poetry Society wasn't offering striptease.

I didn't want the sepulchre of Eros,
huddled with mourners before waxen corpses;
I didn't want to clap with poetasters
the severed head of Orpheus in Earls Court;

in a packed East End pub I drowned my sorrow,
loathing the spill of beer, the reek of breaths,
the vapid babble, brawny men, pale wives –
till from a side-room I heard raucous music.

The young strip-artist was already naked, splayed;
borrowing a bitter and rubbing the froth in,
she caught the drips in the glass, and offered it
with a smile back to the man, to taste, to taste.

He recoiled in disgust; it was too hot a cargo
for these dockers to handle, and they gasped and guffawed
their nausea, yet craned, and stared in awe, as if
at a banana-spider in a crate; as if

this rosy girl with the dark pubic tuft
dripping like woodland foliage after rain
was Salome dancing with the Baptist's head;
even the blacks in our dense standing circle

paled at the gash the strangely innocent girl
was smearing with white. Like great black trees
they swayed away; at the same time their stare
grew rooted in her, as did mine; and when

she put the glass down and resumed her dance,
the writhing girl, straining far back, became
only a medium for what her nakedness
still veiled; and there was nothing in the room

except that hypnotising gash, a part of her
and yet apart; we saw our lives, our deaths;
supported on her hands, her thighs spread wide,
running with sweat, she turned an arc, and gazed

down, with a smile, yet curiously, wistfully,
at the black jolting mound, as if to say −
'I don't know what it is, or where it goes;
it's a rose in a glass, my semi-transparent soul;

it's the place where I have to dance...'
She swayed it like a flute, like the foaming wave
ahead of Venus, wading from the sea −
poetry and striptease, striptease and poetry.

Fox

Thank you for your letter in which you say I shall
    never forgive you but may grow to understand.
You're wrong, though: I forgive you already,
    but I shall never understand.
Your letter was a great shock, as was your 'black book'
    explaining why you think life meaningless.
I wish we could discuss it, at the Turf. I've just
    been sent another surprising memoir − my sister's.
She's finding God in Los Angeles, and still yearning for
    the handsome romantic Texan major
her mother made her give up, on the eve of D-Day,
    for a sensible Australian boy
who wrote nice letters. My sister's just discovered
    sex, too − at 54. Her book is in flexible
red binding and you'd loathe its style, flamboyant and
    inspirational, and even more its message:
'Everything that happens in life is O.K.'
    Well, she's a widow, living alone,
and I don't think her book is meaningless, and
    I don't think your suicide is O.K.

How – on the eve of *your* D-Day – could you compliment
    me so good-humouredly on a new velvet jacket?
Damn you, damn you, Fox! Fox! I never understood why
    your new wife called you that – couldn't see
the likeness; but you foxed her and all of us: working
    slyly for the last fortnight, paying
bills, returning library books, re-directing mail, calling
    on people and places (and cats) who didn't
matter and mattered exceedingly to you. You dropped
    hints, but we thought you were quoting
Sartre or someone – your head thrown back in a short
    manic laugh, you plausible witty bastard.
Oh I grant you a perverse delight in quitting a place
    for good, cramming everything of use into cases
and throwing away the rubbish. To stand in the middle
    of blank walls feels good. But not, surely, when
the stripped room is your life, and you hope and believe
    there is nowhere, and nothing, to go?

I'd like to argue with you your use of the past tense
    in 'having known' me. That was cruel.
I heard you tapping at the window, last night at dawn,
    (though in fact the window was wide open).
You'd like that irony – 'let me back in, it's worse!'
    Fox, how could you forgo the slender girl
under the bough, the flask of wine, the book of verse?
    Music? Cigarettes? – I wanted to look inside
the packet, but dared not, in front of both your wives.
    I guess you miss them, for it's not the calm romantic
sleep you imagined – I hope you're disappointed.
    Now, who will listen to me with such a healing air
of having been there too? On whom shall I depend
    to smoke more, drink more, scatter more debris?
I needed you, more than you knew, so forgive my anger
    (not inconsistent with forgiveness).
I wish you joy and turbulence at your journey's end.
    My friend, my brother, hail and farewell.

Protest

Just and truthful God,
I wish to protest;
there is so much we don't understand,
but you hurry away from our questions
like a politician from the cameras.

Why are the huge eyes of so many children,
too weak even to blink,
opened to your world,
only to become glazed pools
where flies swarm?

Why do you give, to the murderer
of the just ruler, a steady hand,
good luck, fanatical accomplices;
but to the executioner of the tyrant
a clumsy hand, bad luck,
weak and treacherous followers?

Here, an old woman, lonely, wanting death,
pulled alive from the smoking ruins;
there, the young mother of children,
blown to pieces.

Why, out of five of equal aspiration,
do you make one a Mozart, another a Hitler,
another a Kampuchean peasant,
another a rich woman's aborted foetus,
another swept away with millions
in the vaginal fluid?

One a man, another a stoat, another a flower,
another a stone, another – not even a stone?
Any fisherman
who used a net with such wide holes
would leave his family starved.

God, do you ever shudder
with the thought of your non-existence,
as we do with the thought of ours?
With the thought of *why*? Why *you*?
I might have been you,
and you might have been here.

Are you a slave to the dice?

I have a humble place at your table,
but how can I eat your bread,
and drink your wine,
when there are the poor, outside your palace,
stretching their skinny arms through the railings?

Do you envy us our courage, patient endurance,
passion for the unattainable:
qualities you cannot possess?

You are like a quizmaster,
who hasn't himself been given the answers.
You wrap your cloak about you,
your cloak of night and stars.

(After a medieval Armenian poem by Frik)

Sadako Sasaki

who tried to fold a thousand paper cranes
because a crane lives a thousand years
and to fold, with your sick hands, a thousand cranes
would bring back your white cells,

    Sadako Sasaki, twelve years old,
    only a baby when the sun fell in,
    I think of you when
            the nine hundred and sixty fifth
            crane fell from your hands

unfolded, and the sun fell in again.
Somewhere, Sadako, because of you
there are thirty six cranes
flying
            north to their breeding
            lordly
            and crying their cry

    because you were a good girl
    and full of courage
    and wanted life

Sun Valley

It was the first time they had seen the light,
    and gazing, they were too dazed by the sun's
    radiance to murmur when their legs were caught

from under them: with a clean snap of bones
    as they were lifted out, reminding me
    of Yule feasts, or the faint click of a stone's

fall down a chasm. One, that had dropped free,
    was frightened by a ground so fathomless;
    its wings flapped and its legs flopped uselessly.

More fathomless to my vision was the place
    where they were hung up on the hooks that bare
    them swiftly onwards, upside-down in space;

the cause I know not, but all as they hung there
    let fall a rain of excrement, whence came
    the gross miasma everyone must bear.

How weak are words, and how unfit to frame
    my concept – which lags after what was shown
    so far, it flatters it to call it lame!

And it might be ten thousand fowl or one
    went smoothly past the imperceptible
    electric impulse where they had begun

their afterlife, wings fluttering the while;
    and even after they had been thrust through
    the cutter, headless they were fluttering still.

But swiftly after that their power to move
    compassion vanished – as when, journeying far
    down through Inferno, one's own power to love

Vanishes like the sun and the other stars.

Menotti

Menotti is sad because the World Cup has begun,
sad because already they have fallen behind.
Crouched round a wireless in their naked huts,
hearing the frenzy mixed with mountain static,
peasants believe in him, their terrible
faith hunches his shoulders deeper than Atlas'.
Christ of the Andes knows he has no power
to feed the hungry, or to make life bearable.
A mountain as it moves behind the sun
is not more motionless than Menotti.
His face is the mountain looming out of mist
almost touching the wing; and is the night-wind
mixed with moaning in the fuselage;
the steel that finds a home in a girl's breast.
Blood pinks the snow nearby, but otherwise
they're cupped in snowy white on white. Those yet alive
cut into their friend's flesh with slivers of glass
because of the body of Christ, who has ordained
some to die that others stay alive.
The wings! The wings! They're so quick on the break.
Torocsik must be taken out.
A cigarette smokes Menotti to the root.
He's turning into ash.
He's been living for this hour.

Here, in the mountains, stars are moved by love.
On the roof of the Andes, you can see it occur.
You can see God using up his own body
to move the stars. Menotti does not move
a crevice of his stone face, for every time
you move you use up a part of your own body.
Though somehow they've drawn level, he is still
the death-mask. Buried in immeasurable snow,
red nails peep out. They are cutting into her
as they die, praying Our Lady for a miracle.
And they crave stronger tastes, for man is bad.
Send on Bertoni for one last assault.
A centre dies to let a wing survive.

Resting, talking, in the hour before sunset,
watching the peaks crimson, they are almost happy.
You can almost touch God up here. Life is love.
Menotti is sad because his team has drawn ahead.
Above, two condors wheel.
They are the first sign of spring.

Descending on the last of their friends,
and suddenly, round a gorge's bend, more beautiful
than Mary, a patch of green. Keep us on this height.
Wanting to lose, moving the bright stars
over the Andes, as men moved stones to Macchu Picchu.
The ball's passed back again,
possession football. Menotti's face is a tragic
mask at the whistle, but moves like lightning,
sending a smoke-cloud out, a sigh,
embracing his weary and triumphant men.

*Cesar Menotti was manager of the winning Argentine
side in the 1978 World Cup. Other references are to
a plane crash in the Andes in 1972, involving a
Uruguayan rugby team and supporters.*

Elegy for John Walter

(Family-tomb, St Catherine's Church, near Wokingham)

JOHN WALTER
1776-1847

Why, Jack! How goes it, my old chum?
This wedding's got me down; I'm glad
To steal into your shade awhile
Out of the flashy kodachrome.
Steve's cheerful; and the girl's not bad.
Off to Ibiza – not your style.

ELIZABETH ANNE
wife of John Walter
1793-1815
(Dec. 29)

Oh, your young wife, Elizabeth!
Shrouded in her wedding-sheet.
Child on the way, was there? Poor lamb.
The Magi brought her torments, death,
The cold churchyard. Sun-flushed Birgit's
Been fitted with a diaphragm,

MARY
wife of John Walter
1793-1875

Finding the pill had side-effects.
O shit, you might have waited longer.
And yet I'm sure you put it right:
With Mary ageing, loathing sex,
Elizabeth grew ever younger;
I'll bet you screwed her every night.

JOHN WALTER
1818-1894

You're a tough nut, young John in green!
Came kicking through the broken water!
The burden Liza died to bear;
Then, all the joy and half the pain
She left to Mary, like a daughter.
Old lad, you're your own son and heir.

CATHERINE MARY
elder daughter of
John & Mary Walter
1820-1844

Talking of daughters – Catherine
Died just before your father, Jack.
That did for him. She could not face
The hoops of rectitude and sin
(Sickening with a ramrod back),
The hourglass narrowing of space.

EMILY FRANCES
wife of John Walter
1824-1854

Also your third bride, so to speak,
Perished at her Whitsuntide,
Leaving you, precious Jack, aged nine.
Yet she might say, if she could speak,
That she was happy to have died
Before the ape-man's age began.

JOHN BALSTON
eldest son of
John & E.F. Walter
1845-1870

Some say you died a hero's death,
Saving your brother; others write
That, stealing jewels from Sheba's Breasts,
You fell in love, she took your breath
– The sombre bride, the Shulamite,
And in your heart her arrow rests.

FLORA
wife of John Walter
1836-1917

Here, we've a dazed look, slightly grey,
From listening to *our* Zulu spell
– Cranmer's ritual, that nourished
Your Flora through her long, rich day
Until the twilight she timed well,
When all the holy ikons perished.

HUBERT
fourth son of
John & Flora Walter
1870-1933

You scoffed the lot, Jack. What of that?
But Hubert, lucky sod, tight-roped
Between Hiroshima and Mons,
Living discreetly off your fat.
Had Freudian hang-ups, but he coped.
What happened to your other sons?

PHYLLIS
beloved wife of
John Walter
1876-1937

And what – especially – of John?
What did the lad do with his life?
Mortgaged the manor, took the loot?
We only know the bird has flown;
And Phyllis, your beloved wife,
Distressed, sailed off in search, old fruit.

We've swathed into your peace, like rally-drivers,
Clutching our road-maps, burning up your rides;
Fearful that we should find Leviathan
We've goggled round the murky wreck, like divers.
Sleep well, John Walter, with your ivory brides.
We shall not look upon your like again.

For Doll Pentreath
(The last native speaker of Cornish; d.1777)

With the doll she had mothered,
with mother and father,
with boys and maids,

beasts and birds,
curses and songs,
in her crazy old head,

herbs and flowers conferred
day and night-long
around her bed.

All that she loved
in their own tongue
came home and stayed,

and quietly moved
around, as a crone
muttered and prayed

in her simple words,
dying alone.
Cornish obeyed

her, slowly, like the herds
she had driven home.
But the sea bled

back to the whispered
moor-grass and moorstone
of her stone head.

Nothing was heard.
It was home,
where nothing is said.

The Clearing

I make for myself,
or someone makes for me,
a small clearing in my death.
I become a pool
reflecting itself. It is
childhood's pool, utterly clear.

I contemplate it. Who knows
how many years pass?
I look into it, it is full
of sunlight. Who knows
how many years pass?
A waterdrop,

perhaps it is a tear, breaks
the clear water. Circles
spread the pool into
the same pool that turns
into the same pool
and everything the same.
It is childhood's pool, utterly
clear, I am nothing

and I think of nothing.
Once a year I know
it is Good Friday and the pool
is lost. I am broken
into agonised fragments
for three days, then it clears
into the same pool again

and, for a time, something more,
though who it is I am
not certain. I return
to my childhood's pool,
utterly clear. A waterdrop,
perhaps it is a tear, breaks
the clear water, circles

spread the pool into
the same pool, childhood's
pool, I am being cared for
by someone who clearly loves me.

From a Line by Randall Jarrell

Behind everything: all these little villages,
separated by a road, a night, the shafts
of rain my headlights drill
through, and more night, more rain.

They pass without names, without destinies.
Their people are asleep, by twos,
by threes and fours, yet in concord, house
with house. We shall not ever meet.

Yet in each house, in every village,
I sleep, I breathe quietly, I turn, a car
passes, I half wake, and hear the rain,
and travel into the silence, with that man.

The Handkerchief or Ghost Tree

The Handkerchief or Ghost Tree
stands among Monterey Pines,
the Californian Redwood, the Chilean
Fire Bush, the Whitebeam, the Maidenhair.
Tree, in the Garden of Glendurgan
that slopes to the Helford River,
to the quiet beach of Durgan.

I should remember Durgan.
I was taken here as a child,
many times, and the word 'Durgan'
brought joy to my parents' eyes;
but coming here today, carrying
a child in my arms, I can recognise
nothing of this enchanted
estuary. I can remember only
a flash of pebbles, and being carried
in someone's arms.

When my father died,
and I returned to the hospital
to collect his clothes,
I found in the breast pocket
of his laundered pyjamas
a screwed-up handkerchief
still wringing with the sweat
I had watched pour out of him.

Before he started dying,
mysteriously he said:
'My way is clear.'
My sensible Protestant mother
saw a nun, framed
in the bedroom door, warning her
she would always be sleeping alone.

The small child runs
into the garden maze, and vanishes.
We hear his voice, and glimpse
now and again his merry face
through gaps in the laurel.
These lives...these lives that come
and go mysteriously, as the laurel leaves
shine and gloom in the cloudy
sunlight through the tall trees,

this convocation of
the world's trees, massing now
into one, without losing their distinct
character, in the walk down to Durgan.

The Puberty Tree

My puberty tree swayed big, saw-edged leaves
by the open window, and rustled in my sleep
and when I lay awake on the drenched sheet,
for the nights were hot.

I stared at it, whether I woke or slept:
huge black saw-edged leaves against the moonlight.
It pulsed secretly. An immense spider crept
out of it in the dark

and dropped with a light swish into my room:
the Moon-spider, mother of the soft
harmless tarantulas that came inside indeed,
sometimes, and to which

I'd wake in the pale-green dawn or when the fierce
sun was already striking. The puberty tree
spun these black substances out into me,
and also a white

sticky gum I'd find on my chest and belly
in the middle of the night, when my saviour the cool
dawn was a silver-fish in the wall-crack of
a black airless room;

and I lay throbbing, terrified, exalted, strangled,
waiting for the spider-shape to loom.
Night by night the tree went on spinning black
and white substances into me;

now it is wholly inside me: my groin the root,
the slender bough my spine, the saw-edged leaves
my imagination; and the tree sways between
the dark, the light.

Ani

His mother
the earth was very fat,
the terrible and lifegiving milk.
Her voice scolded him, her finger tickled his
little prick, her body pounded maize,
her shadow was pounded.
Dying, she

said, Cut out
the coral-between-my-
legs, and take it to the Island of
Twin Breasts. They will make you a helpmeet.
It was a long voyage. From Ani's
womb they made a plump wife,
and from her

clitoris
a slim geisha. From the
nothing in between they made discord.
His wife found Ani Vaverusa's sea-salt
scent on him one night. She moaned, So that's
why you haven't fucked me
more than twice!

Her lament
upset their two growing
daughters. – I am ill, moaned his geisha,
pushing him off. – Ani Senikumba has
your hut and your children. I'm only
your shell-necklace. – He found
himself tight-

bound between
two straining palm trees. He
had to give Ani Vaverusa
a swollen belly and two wrinkled sagging
udders, and he had to give Ani
Senikumba pearls and
sing her love-

songs. One day
Ani Senikumba
met Ani Vaverusa combing
the beach. They started telling each other some
home-truths. – Old maid, he runs home to me,
and fucks me! – Old cow, this
bundle on

my back is
our son! – Sister! – Sister!
Let's find a sharp flint! – They hurried to
Ani's hut and found him on her bed trying
to get himself erect. Ani! he
shot up ejaculating
milk and fell

back dead. Fruit
of the Distant Sleep and
Flower of the Tangled Root mourned him
on their wedding-day. Ani Senikumba
said, It's going to be lonely, why don't
you move in here with your
little boy?

They live so
close the sun hardly steps
between them. Ani pounds the maize and
Ani sings the beautiful worksong. And when
they cry their shy cries, or laugh, the moon
blushes crimson with the
fun of it.

(from a Fijian myth)

The Myth

My dead father was coming! Thrilled, I said, *Lord!*
I hope I don't run out of things to say,
like when my sister came home, after twenty years,
and I ran out of words, on the drive from the airport.

All the same, my sleep bloomed autumn in winter,
I was dreaming in bronze, while rain was beating my house.
He would love these English colours; and yet, I knew,
New England in the fall was also vivid.

When we met, I told him the good news;
the Reds had beaten Camborne, the old enemy.
Catching a high kick, the blind full-back
burst through to score the winning try.

I was pleased, but not thrilled as I would have been
in the days when we watched together.
Though in some ways I'm still the boy my father
thrilled with the myth of the great pre-war team.

The news was more a way of breaking the ice.
His harrowed face cracked into a smile,
as if he was pleased, but not thrilled;
as if the years made it remote from him also...

When I awoke, I thought much about life
and eternal life, and the blind full-back
racing up by instinct to field the high
garryowen and bursting through to win the match.

Still Life

Each was the Dead Sea of the other's heart,
and the lightning-stroke took pity on them.
For as he turned and stared at the menhir,
the features many years had made unknown
broke again into strangeness and grew clear;
yet when he came back to caress her face
and taste her salt, her features blurred again
to a youthful memory he could not re-trace.
She too, in turning, thought that she still moved
across the plain – and he, the standing-stone
who, as she drew away, grew more beloved,
as though Eve turned again to Adam's bone.

Blizzard Song

On black ice,
lady of secrets,
girl of grey eyes,
we passed each other.

Lady of secrets,
your eyes flicked aside;
we passed each other
but I meant nothing to you.

Your eyes flicked aside
between your upturned collar,
but I meant nothing to you,
you were rushing.

Between your upturned collar
your cheeks were two flames;
you were rushing
to your lover;

your cheeks were two flames; ·
you were bringing heat
to your lover;
passers-by warmed themselves;

you were bringing heat,
scattering show;
passers-by warmed themselves;
smiling through white stars.

Scattering snow,
you stand in his porch,
smiling through white stars
as you slide your coat off;

you stand in his porch,
with the blizzard's song;
as you slide your coat off
we move into one, spinning

with the blizzard's song,
girl of grey eyes,
we move into one, spinning
on black ice.

NEW & UNCOLLECTED POEMS

Sestina: Maria Maddalena

In his Memoirs, Casanova describes amorous encounters with
two nuns, Maria Maddalena and Caterina, at the private casino
of Abbé de Bernis. The scene is the Convent of Murano, Venice.

1

Do my eyes' gazing, Murano master, Jesus,
And my meek up-offered breasts make you too lovesick,
Dim, high on Cross? I'll swear your prick rose!
I, Maria Maddalena, loveliest of petitioning sisters.
O let night come, the pictures, the entwining
Poses, let my breasts swing from nun's blacks free!

2

Time drags. This wearisome chanting!...My ecstatic sisters
Assault you with *aves*. Giacomo never guessed, entwining
His lips with ours. I'll tell him tonight, each rose
Is a prick, is a round window, gives a free
View of us; see how he takes it. Jesus,
The very thought makes me stretch lovesick!

3

All night, spying! My flesh sweats like a rose.
Seraphic, Caterina kneels amidst the sisters,
Her mouth stuffed full with that word Jesus.
Dear, green child! Though, God be thanked, no more lovesick
Of Giacomo: last night's trio made her mind free.
Her limbs with girlish limbs with limbs entwining.

4

Shy to begin – albums, frescos worried her – lovesick
Novice; till 'Which of our breasts please you?' I ask him, and free
Mine; Caterina follows; soon, with blushes, entwining
Happily. All night till dawn we moaned 'Jesus!'
In turn, unselfish, weeping for joy, rose,
Gave place to other, exhorted, were loving sisters!

5

Cruel, your crucified eyes lust, for I am free,
As though you crouched behind the pattern of the rose.
Tomorrow, Giacomo must watch, must crouch lovesick,
Unseen, beholding our rearranged, entwining
Trinity. And last, breathless brothers and sisters,
Do you watch our quartet of joys, I pray you, Jesus!

6

Caterina smiles secretly...Would my lips were entwining
Hers under your horned cuckoldry, Jesus!
One day you will shut our soulful eyes, sisters.
Dust will close up the vulva of each rose.
Giacomo will forget me. Empty will be the lovesick
Casino. Our skulls will lie alone and free.

7

Let nights pass stormy as a crimson rose!
God rot that we should rot here with these sisters!
Send my beauty from God's Leads go free!

Christ on Palomar

I have come out of
the cave, gulped the
thin air, entered
the white
dome

which is more silent, more
laden with awe than
the great temple
of the
prophets.

My brain reels under spectrographs
and maps of galactic
clusters. I was
a simple
carpenter.

Pulsars, quasars and neutron stars.
All such is beyond
me. I thought
only of
love,

creating them. I no longer
pretend to understand my
progeny, why this
particular, chance
design.

Plough, neversetting as the
cells of generation, why
did you sow
so prodigally,
demoniacally?

Andromeda's wheel, you are bland
as a pharisee, luminous,
doublemeaninged, as one
of my
parables.

I know that, if the
faintest star fell or
were added, the
whole would
collapse

like a card-house, but I
no longer remember why.
I bear a
heavier cross
now,

the culpability, the burden of
it all. I am
blinded by the
weight of
stars.

They stream towards me across
fields of space-time, poor
but confident: too
many prodigal
sons.

Persephone

I have seen you wiping tables in the chilly
silent cafeteria of the almost-deserted
railway terminus; and I have seen you in the dim
city street waiting for stranded revellers;
and I have seen you in a nurse's cap
writing letters under a night-light
waiting for disturbed men to cry out for tablets.

And sometimes, when I have lain awake in the dead
of night, it has been enough to imagine you
in these places, knowing that a light still burns
somewhere and that you are awake,
however tired, however slowly you move, however
alone; and that, through you, day runs into day
without a break, the light uninterrupted.

So I am glad you opened your legs to Hades
and agreed to go with him into his dark kingdom,
solid and beautiful amidst the shadows,
our representative presence, childishly fretful,
demanding pomegranate seeds because you are pregnant,
your thoughts rooted in the living,
a white aspen among the black poplars.

Hymen

Catullus, O he licks honey,
cool tar you ran, ay, a genius,
why, rapid, tender and virile,
you decay, then bone, ah, come bone, ah,
    O but alight we go.

Singe the evening with roses,
with suave olives and dancing,
Suneum's cape, light us, seek
seek her venial nipples, lurking,
    let no impediments, come,

now is the vine at ready,
now are the grapes for treading
full as the flesh of Venus
when to her judge's caress
    frigid she flushed clove open,

as a clam, as a flower opens,
as split wood, mortal and tender.
Cleave to the soft axe, cleave
altogether, till the night ends.
    Harbour, us, implicit, errant.

Take, timid, cup in hand, novice,
this petal, dust, amen to that,
star, floss, hyacinth in us,
divide us, dominate, you're too low,
    prod her ass, nova, erupter.

Courage against what ferries
us over purging Lethe,
aeons of our species bring you
to bed, nymph, an irrigation,
    nutrient, human.

Vows in time similar, intact
virgins, you'll quiver but take,
brought home from home, your mothers
weeping and smiling. O hymn of hymnals,
        O home in home are we.

And love enters the audience,
the cither and the drum,
conjugations of mortal,
body venerates body,
        harbour, then, implicit, errant.

This day that's magicest, amazing
is ending, a man to be-
come possessed of the magic
of lightning? O hymn of hymnals,
        O home in home are we.

Your sweet tremulous parents
can't look at, to be virginal
so long it's, but they resign
you timid, you're picked, a novice
        rapt in a glory of marriage.

You're far off, already, in manners,
flowers at your lips, I pull you them,
dead is your dream, you a live
matrix, O hymn of hymnals,
        O home in home are we.

No protest, sign all to Venus,
famished, good, bone, ah, come probe it,
comeliest, capacious, breast,
and violently, who is to know,
        come per air or air or shit.

No law courts will doom us
lips, here, us, dare, no parents
extirpate, tonight, nor protest,
and violently, who is to know,
        come per air or air or shit.

White you are, care for it, sacral,
no disquiet dare preside
in our territory, but quiet,
splendour, potency, coma,
　　　an ardent ingenuous pudor.

Not in tune no need we fear
nature's tenderest, violet
malice, the adulterer,
nor persecuting incubus
　　　will suckle you, bare, the paps.

Lean till, why, feel it, adds to it,
fitted implicit, a harbour, an
implicit arbiter's your plum
complexion, its scarlet dyes,
　　　prod her ass, novel, nuptial.

O you will whatever is human, us

.　　.　　.

.　　.　　.

.　　.　　.

　　　candid our predilections.

Two alight, our pure faces,
flame me then, wider, between here,
run a cool eye, very cool, breast,
I you, O hymn of hymnals,
　　　O home in home are we.

Now from the trees cascading
the nuts will lie where they've fallen,
new juices, the purest, nougats
desserts, at home in me, that audience
　　　of concubines, scatter them.

And whatever is our petition,
bride, cave, never negate us,
nor let us, in everything, eat.
I you, O hymn of hymnals,
　　　O home in home are we.

For you're his home-nest and potence,
and his beata virgin,
quiet in the eye of the storm,
I you, O hymn of hymnals,
　　　O home in home are we.

Loose, mist, set in, at bone, ay,
conjugate, beneath, vivid it,
blueberry, dates, manna,
hungers grow hungers: dying,
　　　wider it won't be rending.

Your honey's spread on us, very,
excite us, we, hilarious, die,
feminine, fuel all I am,
I you, O hymn of hymnals,
　　　O home in home are we.

So, soon, O smiling partners,
manly, O eat vaseline, she is,
flame me then, wide, oven, here,
I you, O hymn of hymnals,
　　　O home in home are we.

Mixed, eyes, bracelets of tears,
you sore, in that lamb, O your breast,
all red, florid, the long night ends,
ah but, such parting's nice, velvet,
　　　float, then, we, together, we're.

Am I right, it's all me you want
silences, where nothing ominous
will, cherish, neck where the vein is,
knee, leg, we'll habituate,
　　　forget to remove your arm.

No dying, commemorate us
a son, vain is the bone to finish
our young desire, when I have passed
concupiscence, love and its offspring
　　　will cap the bone with fire.

Pull over us the chill sky,
cither, drum and the dance
subjugate, numerous prayers
for us to the numberless stars,
      melted and mingled together.

Loaded and livid as berries,
the old men collapse, can't take it,
where they've drunken, dream liberal
young men, easy, slid, undid them,
      simple in again her hairy.

Talking of us, solo, my lonely
mother and her grumbling sleepy
husband tenders us a son
to ride their patrimony on, yet
      semi-resentful her belly.

Sit soon, smiling, in his father's
lap, his face will inscribe
us in the after, humorous
nose, where's that impudence from,
      his mother's, eyes', joy.

Tall as, and strong as ebony,
genius, his mother lauds, approves,
sleeps, quite soon I'll abrupt her,
may try, to let me go, again,
      into her, pineapple, tang.

Frostier, before your sun, virgins:
loose mist set in at bone, ay,
can you guess, beneath, the writhing
moon's your assiduous valentine
      exercising the young men.

(after Catullus LXI)

FROM News from the Front

1

Trench-warfare in my youth: for several weeks
we fought a battle for the virgin soil
under their petticoats, the darkening strips
of nylon; then the bridges that we won
and lost, across the river at whose delta
lay the impossible city. They said, 'You want
too much, too soon...' Their quiet fertile fields
a Passchendaele, it was magnificent
and not really war. And no one lost or won.
Helping to tug that nymphomaniac nun's
tight boots off, then her socks and jeans, I thought
wistfully of that time. The Portuguese
was sliding her unisex briefs off as she slid
into bed. Nuclear blot-out. Jesus Christ...

2

It wasn't enough for her to be the cleft, the night,
the shadow on the universe. That's why
I bit her hard between the thighs, and howled:
trapped in the forest, dragging the man-trap.
It was a bay of worship, of the moon,
which wasn't there. I wanted her to pour
herself into a slender liqueur-glass
like green chartreuse. But would she, fuck.
And yet she wanted me to lie with her
tenderly for a while, the afterglow,
and didn't like me turning on the Bartók.
I switched it off, and did as she required,
smiling and stroking, saying *sotto voce*:
You can't be a woman when it suits you, bitch.

3

It was the same with fetishes: their rage
at seeming to be less important to us
than what they wore. And really we couldn't deny it:
what they wore was more than what they were;
and what their spirit wore, its mask of flesh.
Better Sophia Loren than Mother Teresa,
and better a worn-out tart with painted lips
than Fonda in Vietcong battledress;
we couldn't deny it. Yet they themselves – women –
supposing we could see them as they were,
and love them as they were, would be fetishes
for something less impermanent – the night,
her flying moon, the red-shift of her stars.
Simply there was no answer to the problem.

4

I dreamt of *Liberacion* she'd branded
in a wax model of Sophia Loren.
I knew it was Loren, although the face
was masked, because of the million dollar legs.
We had an argument about the sea
in *liberacion*. From the way dreams go
by opposites, she had left out the sea,
the hungry surge, and the great mother rising.
Who but the mother dominates our lives,
I asked her? Love and wrath! We can't
ever be liberated from her, yet
it's you, you bitches, who do the screaming,
and stick needles in our waxen images,
and forget the original, dreadful, rolling waters.

5

You cunt, the sump, you Kunta Kinte,
you sludge, you slack, you slut, you swamp,
you sac of stagnant water, suck
me in, you cow, you bitch, you *junta*,
you slave, you scum, you poor white trash,
you soil, you shit, you shoe, you tundra,
you coal-forest, you Siberian
meteorite, you gash, you gape,
you stench, you wild orchid, you song,
you sapphire, you muck, you muddy cup,
you clamp, you clutch, you clasp, you clam,
you mum, you *merde*, you bottomless ground,
you hatch, you hutch, you hold, you cave,
you slattern, you hug, you rose, you home,
you cwm, you fallow field, you earth,
you earthenware, you lamp...

6

She hated the word, thought it sounded
even worse than *con*, worse even than her own tongue's
demotic. It was like the venom sucked
out of the cobra's victim and spat away.
We needed a new word. Somewhere
between the hospital and the stagnant swamp
there must be a word like a wild orchid
'beautiful even in our own mirrors'.
But that black vowel, I said, was necessary,
and necessary the harsh crags around it.
Orchids stirred no awe. I wanted Delphi;
cavernous silence, numinous dread. The word
still wasn't obscene enough; I had to have
some curt explosion deeper than all tongues.

7

I saw them in many mirrors, and mirrors
of mirror images: breasts like low hills
when they lay flat, or swaying, hanging gourds;
a brush sweeping through hair; eyes glistening
with tears over a sad part of a book, or widened
to apply mascara; a coat over a chair;
a brassière and one wispy stocking
at the bed's foot. Distillations of women.
The difficulty lay in putting them together
and looking the actual women in the eyes.
Their difficulty lay in looking in mirrors
and seeing themselves there; as a dead summer
might look wistfully at the displays of scent
in windows along the boulevards in autumn.

8

She'd bought a book of erotic reproductions
to take back to a friend. We glanced through it.
I told her she should gaze at her own face
endlessly, like the Rokeby Venus (I slid
my finger down her spine and made her shiver),
because a woman should be narcissistic.
To avoid egotism and melodrama
she should be self-reflecting, and find ways
to be more beautiful. Much better, I said,
than valium. She said, go fuck yourself.
I said the lines of strain could only be
removed by resting on her beauty. Beauty
alone was calm, however wild the breakers
from which she waded, as Velasquez knew.

9

Apart from the shit he talked about Velasquez,
the erotic book we looked at brought us closer.
Strangely, we weren't so very different.
I went for two adolescent lovers embracing,
by Fukui (we both laughed at the name);
and he for a nude girl standing holding a candle
to a surrealist background of a murky street
and a mauve carpet leading up some steps
to a closed door. But everything looked real,
though the girl was sleeping. I was glad
we both liked reality; and I was glad
what turned him on was also beautiful
and even romantic, although the background
to the girl was empty, sombre, geometric.

10

He pointed to the way the sleeping girl's
delicate tuft of auburn hair
haunted the centre of the picture,
stressed by her warm white skin, which in
its turn was stressed by the sombre monotones
behind her. 'And how the auburn of her cunt
is caught up by the candle's flame, and this
is caught up by a small lamp like a moon
down in the street.' When I switched off the light,
his long thin fingers holding a cigarette
were caught in a pale glow
reflected from the wardrobe-mirror holding
a shimmer from the light down in the street.
The swaying curtain lit upon his body.

11

'Of course you've had to fight against the odds.
I'm sure you're right about Florbela Espanca's
poetry, though I've never heard of her
– but then, I wouldn't. And there's Madame Curie,
and Florence Nightingale, and Eva Perón –
amazing, highly creative women. But
is there *one* woman philosopher, composer,
mathematician or even chess-player
you'd mention in the same breath as Descartes,
Beethoven, Einstein, Fisher? Or a playwright
who ranks with – I won't say Shakespeare or Ibsen,
but Noel Coward?...But as you say, you need
positive discrimination for a while...'
I wanted to open the snide bastard out
between the legs and say, That's why, you prick!

12

An agitated voice came through the phone
to me at home. It took me seconds to
remember her. The stupid bitch had lost
her passport, and she wondered if I'd packed it
in my case by mistake. I hadn't done.
Her friend was coming: she rang off. I wondered
how she explained the toothmarks in her breasts
and tracking through the wilderness of hair
on to her olive skin. That crazy night.
And how she loved that lovebite! throwing back
her head, her eyes closed, her mouth wide, as if
she'd crossed some border where I couldn't follow
but where we were, for once, on the same side.

Visions

(a birthday poem for Charles Causley)

At Miller's End, you seem to say,
Dead children live, and speak to us,
And cast their shadows, in a way
The old, though living, cannot do,
Who bear themselves like strips of glass
And scarcely interrupt our view.

We both attend the voice of the bitch
Who harrowed a boy at Botathen farm;
Mother or lover or simple witch,
She did him more good, I guess, than harm:
Unless it is harmful always to crave
The innocent, haunted fields of love.

Ghosts are like bruised, unwanted fruit.
You love them, as you love the poor,
Timothy Winters and Ma Treloar,
Misfits for whom the Master helves
At morning prayers (that's to say – ourselves)...
But tell me who, at Dockacre, plays the flute?

Sometimes, although I know it's his
Bald flute, I imagine it's the wife's sad
Inaccurate tune: the woman shot
Accidentally, or driven mad,
Shut in the dark. I know it's not,
But somehow I still think it is.

In fact, your deceptive, simple song
Weaves them into a common pain.
I like the curled account, in which
He starved her to try to make her sane.
Life, you imply, beyond right and wrong,
Is like the Botathen ghost – a bitch.

Colonel Fazackerley's half-nelson
On that clanking ghost of his is splendid!
The old chap, whose career extended
From – say – a dawn-attack at Ypres
To organising relief at Belsen,
Sees far worse visions in his sleep.

The sailor who walks down Angel Hill,
Like a bronzed, homecoming, emigrant brother;
The boy who says his name is your own,
Down by the quivering stream; the mother
Who leaves the All Souls wine alone –
Are not ghosts, for they are with you still.

And you, although of late you wear
Your hair longer, your years lightly, suits
Suitable for jet-travel, therefore
Are less often in Cornwall than I care for,
Drive all the deeper your dark roots
Into its granite. You are still there,

By the slender, inexhaustible river
Of your childhood, the Tamar that makes us
An all-but-island; still two doors
From the flute-player, the humped moors,
The enigmatic bitch who slakes us
With salt water – Mary the lifegiver.

Writing this under a Christmas star,
I fling, onto the stone Magdalen,
A pebble, wishing she may bless
You with visionary happiness
Still. Change still the water into wine
Like the children at Kfar Kana.

Winchester Cathedral

Where the imperial glory weakly burns
And officers and their wives are high in brass,
Other ranks safely hidden under glass
In a huge book whose pages no one turns,
A Yank, pot-bellied, one of a party, creeps
Around the edge of a perfunctory Mass,
Reflects that everything comes down to class.
'The gooks thought we were rich...' Jane Austen sleeps
Under a slab. A choir in white drag sings.
Pale light through the Jane Austen window falls.
He recalls Nam, a friend whose face peered out
From the gash in his belly, his genitals
Stuffed in his mouth; reflects: There's things
This chick would have found hard to write about.

Muse

I seek a Muse in my new word-processor.
Already she speaks the language of liaisons;
At start of day she springs up like the ocean,
Emerald and translucent, off Porthcurno;
She seems to know by instinct memory's varied
Response to love: some love-affairs abandoned
To Limbo, others forever in the format.

Her heart beats like an invitation: 'Yes?...'
Yet her mind's hidden currents are a maze;
In all my life I've never felt so close
To anyone, yet still with all to learn;
I long to know the colour of her hair,
Which bay or point along her coast to land,
Whether the taking her by stealth or storm

Will open her and let the juices pour;
Whether she's married; has she daughters? sons?
I have to let her run, each line-end an
Impulsive heart-leap; yet at times she's slow
Responding to me, like a caryatid
By the Greek sunlight stunned;
Or like some Renoir girl in a straw hat.

Oars creek; I lean towards her and caress her
Silk cheeks; I feed her red lips dates and raisins;
Light glistens on her shoulders like a lotion;
I offer her closed teeth a sip of Pernod;
The bank is streaked with flowers that die unmarried;
A water-lily touches her trailed hand, and
Ephemerids are dancing in a swarm at

A spot where a tree's bark and wayward tress
Are blended into one by the sun's rays;
She's innocent of the highlights on her nose
And forehead that at suppertime will burn;
She doesn't feel the hovering insect where
Her perspiration mixes with a strand
Of hair; the model's drowsing in the warm

Flesh-tones of images she knows before
I do; verse faster than the spider runs
Across the water; for her dreaming scan
Instantly persuades her where to flow.
She wouldn't know it if my fingers slid
Under her dress; her breasts are damp with sand
From swimming earlier, the nipples flat.

Freed to the air, they warm to the sun's laser
Yet remain tranquil, like inverted basins.
Does she exist, this lady whose emotion
May span the Paradiso and Inferno?
She isn't answering my calls; I'm worried;
Something I said, she failed to understand? An
Imploring telegram lies on her door-mat.

Here

I'm here. I wasn't sleeping, only drowsy;
I felt your fingers, they were not unwelcome,
But you must understand that I'm still fearful,
Being newly-born, or suffering amnesia
– I don't know which. This whole storm-driven summer,
My first perhaps, you've trusted me. I thank you.
Your life has flown in like a flock of starlings.

Yet all I know is what your touch allows.
You are the sea, and I your faithful shell.
I only hear the words you let me hear...
Ballerinas sway like winter trees...
Does that mean anything? Why did it come?
They stand, in slim skirts, at a taxi-rank,
Perhaps...will soon be travelling, travelling far.

A transatlantic flight...It's come to me –
The women stand in some
Queue at an airport. Ah, my mind's like wool;
All I can do is give you what you saw,
And you saw winter trees sway and confer.
I've been confused like this all summer through.
They sway so gracefully they might have wings.

The horizon's line of birches might be flying...
Such memory-images break up the darkness,
If they are memories and not your creation.
You smoke a cigarette and sit in silence,
Recalling your past life – mostly with sadness;
I don't know why, since you remember singing,
Laughter and beauty. You're too avaricious

For happiness. In my experience I
Would say life's like a flood, and there's no ark.
You're born, you rapidly grow up, you mate,
Follow your ancestors in single file.
Count yourself lucky if you don't go mad.
I may be wrong. I don't know anything.
I'm just a shell, a listener, like a dish

At Jodrell Bank, hearing the cosmos ring,
While I don't even know my own address.
Who's calling us, the Father or the Son?
An obscene caller? Is it making sense?
I only speak in jagged terms unless
You guide my thoughts and bring
An ordered cosmos flying in to us.

These tall slim ballerinas flying, drowsy,
Cover their eyes with masks and welcome darkness
Droning above the world's creation, fearful.
Around them lost souls sleep. Amnesia. Silence.
I seem to feel already a sadness: summer,
And as it were the insects' thank-you, singing
To those that eat them, avaricious starlings.

The World's Creation

You say, we're sailing on a ghostly ship
And we don't know whose hand is on the tiller.
You're early-wise, my bride of Frankenstein;
Where did you get your knowledge of the world?
I seem to see you in a rushing sleigh:
Red cheeks, white teeth, fur hat, your blond hair streaming
– You show too much experience for a child.

You smile as you exclaim, 'The world's fucked-up!'
Ah but, my dear – Marya or Liudmila –
There's one sweet consolation – no, not wine,
Though it looks dewy, like a rose infurled,
Sketched, in *The World's Creation*, by Courbet –
A vulva floating free, as if it's dreaming,
Still fresh enough to breathe a scent, so mild

The climate. Fleck our steeds with a light whip!
I know a country, called by Henry Miller
The Land of Fuck. There, all lives entwine,
And on the storm of their delight are swirled.
There the deep midnight meets the start of day,
The faintest glow-worm meets the comet beaming,
Unicorns are by ladies' laps beguiled.

The gravest poets have enjoyed their trip
To the Land of Fuck: Goethe, Wordsworth, Schiller,
Dante and Milton. For the journey's fine
– Even the journey, through the ether hurled,
So that, although the country moves away
As you approach it with the horses steaming,
The distant sight of it can drive you wild.

A country without frontiers, you can slip
Into it with the lucky girl and fill her
With untaxed liquor from the purest vine,
A blend so potent that straightway you're curled
Up warm within the harvest that some dray
Is carrying to market. The driver's scheming
A profit for himself; bale upon bale is piled...

Yet there are badlands, where you're made to strip
– I ought to warn you – by cold-blooded killers;
A knife pricking your throat, you're bound with twine
And ransacked for a gold coin or a pearl.
With seven veiled wives a lunatic holds sway;
There the deep forests lie, with brigands teeming.
No one has gone there without being defiled.

– So it is said. I heard it from the lips
Of a *rusalka*, daughter of a miller,
Who trawls all seas from Dnieper to the Rhine
Seeking revenge, by waves and fury whirled,
An infant on her back. But we shan't stray
Far from where, by that World's Creation gleaming,
All violent anger's straightway reconciled.

A Guide to Switzerland

The mountains write our only history
In a white calligraphy loping between horizons;
We live in such a stunning snow-silence
We could never make history happen,
It could only happen to us; like Poland, like Russia.
Who'd want statues of Eternal Memory,
Eternal flames flickering between black marble?
Enough innocents have died on the flanks of Mont Blanc.
History is
A January morning of unusual warmth
Melting snow, closing the ski-runs.

We have no art. Who wants
The tortured canvases of Goya and Van Gogh,
The miseries of Anna and Vronsky? Madame Tussaud
Was a famous Bernese lady.
We have no eyes. You will not find
The painfully wrinkled eyes of old Greek peasant-women,
Nor the fiery black eyes of their granddaughters;
We prefer the solid whispers of bank-notes,
The placid Monopoly of our neat gabled chalets,
To the passions of an Yseult, an Isadora.

We make the watches
That tick away the moments till dawn
For sinful foreign lovers;
We live in the unproblematic future,
A peace the world outside us dreams of achieving;
But don't imagine it doesn't take courage
To live without neurosis.

Transatlantic Greetings
(for Diana Der Hovanessian)

We reach what our forefathers knew as Christmas;
Three rich kings ride on my accountant's card.
New wives prepare traditional menus, stocking
Larders and cabinets. I join the mass
Of late-night shoppers fighting for goods in
A musak'd store; which record would be right

For my stepdaughter? – the Beethoven Mass?
Madonna? Our rituals, adrift from Christmas,
Are making-do, like a bride's white silk stocking
Tied as a fan-belt. In Bethlehem, the inn
Is being searched for bombs primed for the rite
Of wine turning to blood. Somewhere a card

Explodes in someone's face. Diana, write,
Over and over, your country's Requiem Mass,
You'd never reach the last, bloodied discard,
A people peeled off casually as a stocking,
Under Mount Ararat. As Christ at Christmas,
Ignored, forgotten. No room at the inn.

Her face almost a stranger's in the mass,
I bump into my ex-wife... 'It's all right...
Nothing is perfect...Thank you for your card...
I've bought a few things for my stepson's stocking...'
Is this the face eternal, once, as Christmas?
'I must go. Nice to see you.' She's lost in

The blur of coats and parcels. Nothing's right;
Love comes like the apologetic card
In time for the New Year. I'll spend this Christmas
Mourning the years that fluttered down *en masse*
From a child's joy, a bolster for a stocking,
And sleepy, murky parents flitting in.

Your daughter will be home? – A royal card.
You'll offer a New England-Armenian Christmas,
Sipping no more red wine than at the Mass,
Tipsy with simple love. I see you in
Your street of vested scholar and bluestocking,
As calm and passionate as the verse you write:

Striving to find a language for our stocking-
Masked, brutal century; translating Cambridge, Mass,
To stony cities you're proficient in.

A Literary Lions

Tolstoy has got to be your full-back, flawless
Defensively, then surging up with raking
Strides in attack; perhaps a shade pedantic,
Less nimble than the author of *Spring Torrents*,
But massively secure, like a Caucasian
Peak. Now for your wings; pick someone who is
Deceptively slight and seeming-vague, a dreamer,

Yet with the sudden pace to warm a raw
Day into flame and leave a poignant ache:
Shelley – by no means such a sensitive plant;
Your other great wing, one who's bound to score
As he scoops up a pass with classic grace,
And rouses ecstasy as he glides through
A packed defence: Catullus. Mix a gleam

Of genius with sound judgement under stress
At centre. Joyce would be magic; Fielding
Would give good English value, nothing slick,
Wind fanning his long mane, an upright stance.
And as their fly-half, Emily Dickinson;
She makes space for herself, and like a breeze
Dummies and feints – they would be tackling her

While Joyce was clean away, Emily ball-less,
Or they'd be grabbing him while she was breaking.
Scrum-half? I would say Pushkin; with his antic
Whims he's less predictable than Lawrence;
Dream of a service, and the right occasion
Will see him grab the ball and wriggle through, as
Ghostly and untouchable as a lemur.

Your props? George Eliot and George Bernard Shaw?
Okay; with Zola hooking, yes – or Blake:
Demonic, though a shade inelegant,
Someone who knows the lineaments of a whore
And also has a hooker's flattened face.
That front-row would be tough as old boots; you
Won't punch or head-butt them. Christ, what a team!

Wordsworth in the second-row? I guess
I can just see that, torn shirt fluttering
And bald head stained with sweat, though he's a prick.
Shakespeare – of course, freezing into a trance
All line-out jumpers with his vaulting span;
And you're quite right to make him captain – he's
Prospero with the tones of Warwickshire.

Wing-forwards should be vagabonds, pure lawless
Energy: can't you see Villon, flaking
Off from the scrum? Then brooding, necromantic
Dante, I think, wreaking revenge on Florence;
And finally, a powerful and half-mad Asian,
His hands like naked swords, ready to spew his
Guts out for his honour's sake: Mishima.

In the Fair Field

In the fair field
studded with tiny flowers
swayed by a wind
your green skirt stirs.

Studded with tiny flowers,
green voyager,
your green skirt stirs,
whispers.

Green voyager,
the grass
whispers,
and we turn with the earth

the grass
as the clouds turn slowly
and we turn with the earth,
and someone is saying,

as the clouds turn, slowly,
'my sister'
and someone is saying
'my friend'.

My sister
is that a bird's fluttering?
My friend
do you feel presences?

Is that a bird's fluttering
in the tight throat?
Do you feel presences,
a ghostly celebration?

In the tight throat
my soul shivers
a ghostly celebration
running through grass and flowers.

My soul shivers,
swayed by a wind
running through grass and flowers
in the fair field.

Index of titles and first lines

(Titles are in italics, first lines in roman type.)

D.M. Thomas was born in Redruth, Cornwall, in 1935. In an area rich in tinmining history, his family had been miners or craftsman working in the mines. He was educated at Redruth Grammar School and at University High School, Melbourne: his parents emigrating to Australia in 1949, following their daughter's marriage to an Australian serviceman. Returning to Britain in 1951, Thomas spent most of his National Service learning Russian. His instructors graded him 'suitable for low-level interrogation after further training'. He has never interrogated anyone, but has used his Russian to translate the poetry of Akhmatova and Pushkin, and has been profoundly influenced by Russian literature.

He read English at New College, Oxford, where he was awarded a First. He taught for four years at Teignmouth Grammar School, and simultaneously began writing poetry. His first publication was an Outposts pamphlet, *Personal and Possessive* (1964). He became a lecturer in English at Hereford College of Education in 1963, eventually becoming Head of Department. 1968 saw the appearance of *Penguin Modern Poets 11*, with a selection of his poems, and *Two Voices* (Cape Goliard), his first collection. Four more collections followed, culminating in the highly-praised *Dreaming in Bronze* (Secker & Warburg, 1981), for which he received a Cholmondeley Award. His latest poetry book is *The Puberty Tree: New & Selected Poems* (Bloodaxe Books, 1992).

In 1978, he decided to write full-time. He had begun to explore fiction, and his first novel, *The Flute-Player*, won the *Guardian/Gollancz Fantasy Prize*. His third novel, *The White Hotel* (1981) became a critically acclaimed and controversial bestseller. Translated into twenty languages, it won the P.E.N. prize, the *Los Angeles Times* Fiction Prize, and was a Booker Prize nomination. His subsequent quintet of novels, *Russian Nights*, takes further his attempt to find a fictional form based on improvisation, in which poetry, prose fiction, drama and memoir can all find a place. His most recent novel is *Flying in to Love* (Bloomsbury, 1992), an exploration of John F. Kennedy's assassination. He has published a memoir, *Memories & Hallucinations*.

In 1987 Thomas returned to his native Cornwall. He has two sons and a daughter. He lives in Truro with his second wife and their teenaged son.